MY BLESSED GARAGE

By: PJ Warrior

Dedication:

My amazing husband,
I love you with both my hearts

My awesomesauce daughter,
Ollie Ollie ~ We're Free!!

CONTENTS

INTRODUCTION

I have had a tough time writing this introduction page. I guess that's because I've never really read the intro pages to books (I know, don't judge me) and not sure how to keep you here long enough to read mine.

To be honest, I didn't want to write this book at all, and I for sure never wanted to publicly share the most devasting thing to happen in my life. So, why did I write this? Because I don't want marriage to be a coin flip! We live in a world where marriages literally have a 50/50 shot at making it, and honestly, I was almost on the wrong side of that coin flip.

From the last twenty years of Bible study and learning, I realized something. None of it matters! It's true! Not one bit of it matters unless you are truly willing to Walk the Walk you so boldly Talk about!

Meaning, when the war comes, are you really going to: Put on Love and Get Out Of Your Boat. Will you actually Walk in a Divine Direction. When it's all said and done, will you like the Sum of your Decisions?

I have been raised by two amazing preachers for over twenty plus years. The war did come, and I had to make a choice. I had to decide if I would 'for real' Walk the Walk of a true Christian, or I was just full of hot air and only Talk my Talk.

I know right! It's all fun and games until God steps in and tells you to do something that every fiber in your body does NOT want to do.

I did it though! I fought the war with all I had, and I won!

I wish there were no other marriages out there facing what I faced, sadly I know that's not true. I am hoping to reach that woman or that man who now sit in the very spot I did.

That place in your marriage and life where you're so destroyed, and yet, you know that you know, God is telling you to stay.

But How?!?

I hate typing these words, but the story you are about to read all happened because my husband desperately tried to cheat on me.

There was only one problem with that plan. My husband forgot one small little sentence that my mother said to him the very first time she met him over thirteen years ago.

My mom said, *Don't ever doubt my daughter's connection to God.*

You see, I have been talking to God like I'm talking to you now since I was five years old. It's a story my mom loves to tell, and maybe one day you'll hear it from her, but for now let's just say, my husband didn't stand a chance in his little plan!

My life has been a non-stop battle for over forty years. Yes, I may have had God in my life since I was little, but it didn't mean it was ever easy. I have a very dark childhood, but the one thing I have never wondered is....Does God Love Me.

My *passion* in life has always been working with teens that others have forgotten and thrown away. However, I have now found what my *purpose* is in life. And that purpose is, to change the coin flip stats on marriages!

I sincerely have only one goal for this book.

I want to help you take your life back from those stupid voices that have been lying to you!!

To get what I *need* you to get out of this story. You must first stop, breathe, and then erase everything you have ever been told or taught about God, Jesus and being a Christian.

Not forever silly, just set it aside for a couple of hours. Clear your head and go back.

Oh come on dude, go back further than that! I mean go way back to when you were a child, back to that time in life, when you could simply - *Believe.*

I'm serious, if you do not empty your head of all the information you have been given over the years about being a Christian, then you will miss this moment.

I can't explain how to do it; I'm not in your head, *yet*.

But *you* can go back to that time way back when.

Do you remember when you believed that you could run to the end of a rainbow? Ever wonder as a child if one day you could fly? Remember when you were little running around in the back yard trying to catch those magical fireflies? Can you remember that time in your life when you simply believed that God was real?

Ya! Go back to that time and place, please.

Clear your mind clutter and *listen* to my story. What you are about to read *will* sound way out there and way past what you think you can *believe*.

But isn't that precisely what we are told to do? SIMPLY BELIEVE?!?!?!

Matthew 18:3 ... Truly I tell you, unless you change and become like little children, you will never enter the kingdom of heaven.

Dude! You have to *Tilt Your Head A Little*!! You're looking at this world all wrong!

For real! Hang out with me for a little while and let me tell you who my cool Father *really* is.

MY BLESSED GARAGE

How do I even explain what you are about to read? I guess the easiest way to explain it is that, you are about to get a 'tiny glimpse' into the worst and most painful moment in my life.

Why? Because God told me to, and no matter how much I tried, and trust me! I tried NOT to do this, but the words kept spinning in my head, and I could hear my Father asking me to get moving forward.

My first reply was, *No thank you, I don't want none of that.* He persisted, and well, here I am.

As I type these words, I do have to admit that I'm becoming curious, scared, a little bit excited and again scared, as to what God's up to this time.

Isn't that the way it usually is with God? You get a little puzzle piece here, then another over there until eventually, it all starts to make sense. Would you also maybe agree that when it all gets a little confusing, more times than not, we walk away from whatever God is trying to tell us?

I know I use to. I would get upset at the puzzle piece information He was giving me at random times, feeling like some weird coded message.

Confused, I would walk away and carry on with my own plan.

Now, many years later, I do understand a little more why He does that. No, I can't explain why He does it that way, sorry. I just know that I know - He ALWAYS has my back!

So, where did this funky art come from?

That's actually quite a long story, and really in full circle, it's the whole point of this writing, don't worry we'll get to all that later. The story unfolds as each painting is introduced, so we have plenty of time.

I will remind you that I said you get only a TINY GLIMPSE into my world. The paintings are really in-depth storyboards, and so much information just isn't possible to explain here. It's a story that is told as I need to, but if you are looking for a full dump of my life, over the absolute worst thing that ever happened to me, all right here? Oh, that's funny! I don't think so dude.

The story is out there, it's not a secret, and when it needs to be told, God places the people in my path.

I hope you don't quickly judge me as others have before by thinking, *Oh ya, good for you having your life all together and able to sit in a garden all day and write.*

I didn't get this life by 'wishing upon a star' – I got this life by having a backbone and by fighting desperately for over twenty years to escape my horrible past and holding to a promise of a better future.

Then, I was stalked by demons & guarded by angels.
Now, I am guarded by angels & stalking demons.

I finally got it!! I didn't only figure out how to play this jacked up game called LIFE - I also figured out how to flip the tables on those stupid voices in my head, the ones that have tried to take my life since I was only ten years old. I started fighting for my life at a very young age, a long hard fight that took almost forty years to unfold into a full-blown war.

When the war came, I did fight back and won in a HUGE way! And now I help others to take their lives back! Not only to live and survive in this world, but how to be truly HAPPY living here.

It is possible! It's not an easy path to start down, but if you really want a better life, and you're fed up of only surviving in this crazy world, then maybe, just maybe, we could be closing in on the reason you're reading this right now.

WHO ARE YOU ANYWAY

Who am I? Well, the simplest way to put it is; I'm a country girl from the Mid-West ~ raised on a front porch ~ princess warrior daughter of God.

I don't have any fancy letters after my name, I'm not rich nor do I have expensive things. So, I guess by any worldly standard, I'm nobody.

However, the actual truth is, quite a few people in my world think I'm a lot weird (which is a great compliment) and they see me as a person who honestly does know what side is up in this upside-down world.

I can't explain why, how or what happened that made God use these oddly amazing paintings to talk to me in my little garage. All I know is that my life, home, and marriage was saved from ruin. Not only did I get my life back, I got it back better than it was before. I absolutely got back way more than just double for my trouble!

It was not easy, and unfortunately, I have to confess one small detail. I had to commit murder to get it all back.

But then again, if you had the life I have, you'd murder to take it back too!

If you wanted to stop reading at my earlier mention of "God" – I'm glad you didn't, and I promise you, I'm not 'that' Christian. You know the one(s) I'm talking about, that so-called Christian that hurt you by judging you or the one that made you feel as though God wasn't able to love someone like you. Maybe a church made you feel unwanted. I don't know, but you're obviously reading this for a reason. Who knows, if you hang out for a minute, you just might like being in my weird world.

You really have to understand that there's so much more than just what happened in spring 2017. You're about to take a quick ride through only two short years of my life.

That means, in order to get you caught up to the current time in my world, you kind of need to hear the set-up of my life to even be able to understand the punch-line that is coming later.

I sigh deeply as this part isn't fun at all. I'm going to give you a 'sprint through' version of my life from age four – age twenty-three in let's say five seconds?

Ok, just breathe girl, type it, dump it out into the deep dark world of judgment and just, let it be...

I lived with my DNA grandma until I was four years old. I then moved to a new family at five years old (*I was adopted by a personal family friend, so I grew up knowing both family sides*).

Since age five, I have been an emotional yo-yo for most all family members on either side of the DNA & Adopted world. I was sexually abused by multiple people starting at age five, continuing until age twelve. My first suicide desire/request was at age ten.

Age fourteen I ran away and hitchhiked all the way across the USA with truck drivers (ya, smart one right).

I moved out of my home at the young age of fifteen.

Oh hold on dude, it's just getting started.

I was married at sixteen, not married at seventeen. Drinking by fifteen, drugs by seventeen.

My world was a horrid mess by age twenty. Suicide request/attempt number two at just age twenty-three.

Age twenty-three I was broken, lying alone on the bathroom floor. I cried out to God, begging Him not to leave me where I was, and my loving Father RAN to me.

I've been chasing after His heart ever since.

Let us please make one thing clear. This was a little what, five maybe a ten second sprint through my life? It was so much darker than these pretty little typed letters, but that's all for another time. I'm just trying to explain in short that I do know what troubles are in life.

It's also very important to understand that what happened in the story I am about to tell is all linked. It is linked to my past, linked to my life choices and linked to all my past decisions. It all led to this place right here in my life.

Now creeping into my late forties and over twenty years of real Bible study, I'll admit that I'm still learning and fighting to get home every single day. Thankfully, I now understand what those stupid voices in my head have been trying to do to me and in my life for all these years.

Oh ya buddy, and with that revelation. I flipped the tables!! Those stupid demons are no longer stalking me, I'm stalking them!!! And you know what? I'm getting better at it with every battle and war that I fight!

THE STORY PICTURES

I've never done any sort of art stuff before this. I'm creative ya sure but painting? Haha, now that's funny! I tried to paint once with my grandma years ago in my early twenties. My grandma was a fantastic painter, but me? Oh Lord have mercy, I once painted a unicorn that looked like a cat, that ate a dog and then was possibly kicked by something, but by no means, did it look like a unicorn.

So, where did this funky art stuff come from anyway? The short, simple answer is; this is what happened when God had to tell me a secret in my garage.

If you're trying to figure out just what's going on here, I can understand that, please hang in there a little longer, it will all start to make sense. At least I hope so.

I mean really, what happened in my simple little world was so insane that I've struggled ever since to make it into understandable terms within my own head, much less, explain to someone else in believable words.

And when I do have to talk to someone and tell a little about what happened, I freeze and fear sets in almost instantly. Why? I don't like being judged and Lord help them, but even those with the best intentions do judge. Some people look at me funny, and others straight up don't believe any of it.

I don't know what to tell ya dude, but it's only fiction if it didn't happen!

So, believe what you will. All I know is, if I can get even one spiritual seed to land out there somewhere, I'm happy.

In all the crazy that happened, I am still amazed at what God made using my hands. I had no clue what to do, just tucked myself away in my garden and little garage listening to Him telling and showing me everything I needed to know about a war that was unfolding behind the scenes of my life and world as I knew it.

You have to remember, as I mentioned on the Introduction page, I've been talking to God like I'm talking to you now since I was five years old! God had a very special reason for doing it that way, and I am forever grateful.

That first day in my garage, I was confused and scared, but of what? Why was I feeling so afraid?

I prayed and asked, *God what are these jerks trying to take from me this time?*

I got only a one word answer from above...

Everything...

WHEN YOU HAVE THE RIGHT

Sorry, I'm not trying to stall in telling my story, I just need to ask you a very important question first.

What would you do if you had the right to walk away from a relationship, from a friend, family member, or even a marriage?

I mean the *right* to walk away? You could walk out the door and leave the damage behind, all with a clear conscience.

When your heart has been ripped out of your chest and handed to you from the very person you needed and expected to be loyal, what would you do? You walk away, right? Yep! I agree, and that's just what I *tried* to do.

The tree climbing, horseback riding, Mid-West country girl ragged inside and I was one step away from closing the door of the relationship. And that relationship I'm speaking of? Well, that would be my marriage of almost thirteen years.

Not a bad marriage either, that is what's so crazy! We are very close, best friends, always been on the honeymoon if you will, all good right? I mean I'm Christian, and he's Christian, so we're evenly yoked, yes?

Uh, are you sure about that? It turns out that for the last thirteen years, I've actually been married to and living with a Christian Atheist!

My husband had gone another path quite some time back, and I hadn't even caught it. It's always a *slow fade* my friend. Homes, families, and people never fall apart in just one day!

It's a series of choices, each choice or compromise you make adds up.

Why? Because you are the sum of the decisions you make! Bad decisions will always come out... bad.

So, problem solved right? Walk away and burn it all to the ground?!? Well, not quite. What if you try to walk away from the relationship with all your rights in hand and God requests that you stay?

I mean when God tells you straight to your heart.... *I need you to stay and love them through this.*

Uh, then what do you do? If you're anything like me, then your reply to God will be very similar to mine...

Oh, I'll love them Lord! I'll love them with the front of my car- then I'll love them again with the back of my car.

Screaming out to God and demanding that JUSTICE be done.

Well, hold on tight my friend because God will sometimes take you DIRECTLY into the fire just to see what you will do. Question is, will you be able to hear His soft voice through all your *rightful* rage? Will you trust God enough to take care of you and your situation?

When the pain is beyond anything you have ever imagined, will you believe He will protect you? Or will you do like you have done before by taking matters into your own hands, and go forward in search of the justice you so rightfully deserve?

Don't misunderstand me! Sometimes the answer is simple: GET OUT! I know that to also be true, I've been there. I mean seriously, we really do get ourselves into some humdingers of messes right?

There are times when you are to walk away, but I'm talking about that situation when, *you know, that you know,* you're supposed to stay, but how? How can you ever forgive and move on? How will you ever find yourself again, much less be happy?

SELF-WORTH

The first day I was placed out in my garage by God, I was mad, country girl mad! I was confused and flippen my lid as to what I was feeling inside, and my stomach was in the worst knot ever. To make matters worse, I was also clueless. How to even start with a painting? I mean do you go middle, side, top or bottom?

I was holding a box cutter at the time, and I could feel my anger rising. I yelled out, *Fine! You want me to paint!*

Then I raised the box cutter knife up over my head, and brought it down hard, right in the middle of the canvas, and ripped it I did.

Well, after I cried for a while, and finally calmed down, God said to my heart, *Ok, now that you're finished, please fix it.*

I popped off, *Fix it? Seriously? There's a huge rip in the middle.*

He gently repeated, *Fix it.*

I kicked rocks for a minute, but I finally did get it (okie rigged) fixed.

And that simple argument, and raw honest moment with God, set the whole painting series and painful story into motion.

God literally went to hell and back with me to save my life, my home, and my world as I knew it.

Now when someone asks me what this painting is, I just smile and say, *That's what I'm worth to God right there on canvas.*

God tucked me away for the coming next weeks in my garden and little garage. He talked, I listened, I also cried, I begged, I fought and then I listened some more. I listened to Gods calm voice and did what He told me to do. It wasn't easy, and many days I kicked rocks, while other days I straight failed my test.

This wasn't something that just happened overnight. No, this started way back in time. Those sneaky demons had been quietly working in the background, grooming the situation of my marriage, just waiting for the perfect moment to strike.

The showdown did come. High noon stuck and when God said to stand up and fight, I obeyed and did! I drew my sword and ran straight to the battlefield.

I fought with everything I had in me, blood was shed, demons were slain and scattered across the living room floor.

And me?
Well, I was hurt worse than ever before.

Was it worth it?
Stick around and you tell me...

LOVE IS A 4 LETTER WORD

Oh Lord, ain't that the truth! For the most part, that word is kind, nice, fair, pure.

Sometimes though, that word is lies, pain, rage or even FEAR.

Within a few days and things are quickly changing in my world. And trust you me, love was anything but a word right now in my home. I still had no idea what to do with these weird paintings that were forming in my little garage, or why I was even doing them. Part of me was genuinely amazed at how talented God was, as I knew full well it wasn't me making these odd yet beautiful paintings. What I couldn't wrap my head around was...why? Why was God making me stay in this garage for hours every day, what was He trying to tell me and when or even how was I ever going to figure out what these little puzzle pieces meant?

It was all a hot mess in my home, and my head was starting to spin almost daily as new developments came to light. Each day the crazy was becoming more evident and to be honest, it all just sucked!

I had no idea what to do and all (I felt) God had me doing was roaming around in my garden picking up stupid little sticks, gathering flowers, small tree limbs, evergreen pieces, old junk laying around, plaster for filling holes, glue, paper towels, wire pieces, newspaper and a LOT of lacquer paint.

I was still trying to convince myself that nothing was wrong, and I decided that I wanted a pretty and bright painting, one that was full of color. It started out fine, and I was having fun mixing colors to see what happened. But no matter how colorful I made it or how much I tried, the word FEAR just kept showing up on the painting. It made my stomach drop every time it was placed on there. I would change it to letters that spelled out Love, Kind, Hope, but each time I did, God would again request that it be put back to the word FEAR.

Well, after the second or third time, I snapped inside. I had had enough, and the little five year old princess in me came shining out in all her glory and with nothing short of throwing myself down on the floor and flailing my arms.

I started off with my rant.

Stop it already God! I do NOT want that WORD on there! I wanted a light and fun painting! You know what? I don't even like this painting anymore. It's not the way I want it. Honestly, I don't even know what I was thinking in the first place! I don't paint. This is just stupid, and on and on...

Sadly, that went on for some time, but I finally did calm down, eventually giving in and doing as I was told by placing the letters F-E-A-R back on the painting.

Then, of course, like any ticked off five year old, I covered the word FEAR with three layers of different colored paints, textured over it, glued things on it, by it and around it. But no matter what I did, God kept on letting that word FEAR come bleeding through.

When I finally did *for real* calm down and apologize, something amazing happened.

You have to understand something. I was hurting yes, but I wasn't mad *at* God. I was mad at what was going on around me, my pain was becoming unbearable, and God was the *only* one I had in all of this. He actually made sure of it!

Meaning that, I tried to turn to a girlfriend, but we never could connect with each other. I tried to talk to a family member, but was never able to get together on the phone.

God needed me alone with no outside interference. Sometimes, being in a private place is best, and it's always wiser to - Go to the *Throne* before you go to the *Phone*!

Did you even know that you can argue and yell with God? It's true! I've been doing it since I was a little girl and it's not only true, He actually *appreciates* it when you go straight to Him with your issues. He will let you kick and yell, and even throw a fit, but then you must stop and listen.

He is usually just waiting for us to calm down long enough to be able to hear Him. Once I finally calmed down, then and only then, could an awesome moment happen between me and God about my painting.

He said gently, *Tilt your head princess. You're looking at it wrong.*

It was awesomesauce cool then, and it still gives me love chills writing about it now. It was a moment just for me, special from Him, reminding me how much He loves me.

What did I see when I tilted my head? I saw my promise. I saw my caring Father reminding me of the promise He made to me one very important day long ago when I was a little girl crying in my tree.

Right now, more than ever, I needed to be reminded of that promise. I needed all the strength I could gather for what was coming my way. I still had no clue yet what was happening or why it was necessary to God that I stay in this garage.

I foolishly thought I was going into a battle, only to find out, I was at the beginning of a war.

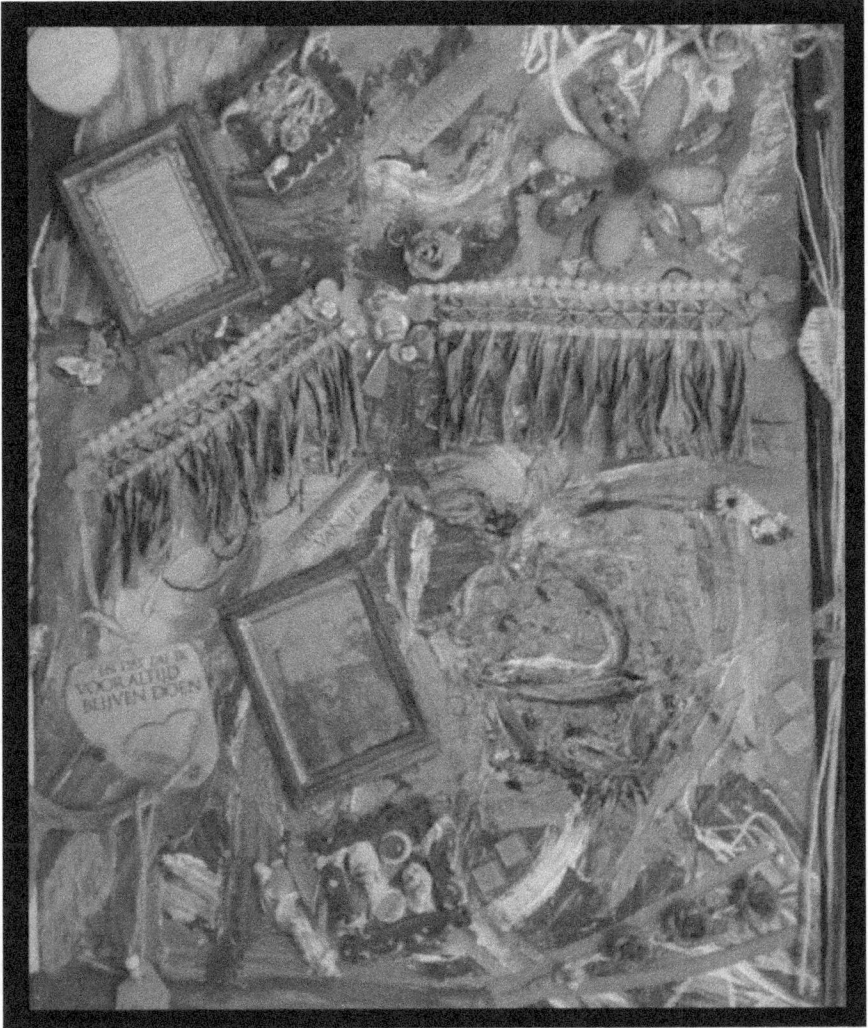

WARRIOR

Well, by now I was heading straight down the main road into crazyville.

No seriously! I mean hot chicky day dude, I was turning around at every moment saying to myself, *What in the world is going on*!!!

I didn't know what to do. I could see things, but I was seeing it way different than anyone else around me. I felt like I was the only sane person, and constantly thinking, *Can no one else see this horrid mess*?

My husband is saying and doing things right in front of my face which are literally making my head spin. And by now, *I know, that I know, that I know*, my husband is up to something. I was finding things out at a fast pace, and it was all starting to come to light. In my garage that is! Each day, God was telling me more and more secrets.

And even though it was only a short time now living in this twisted altered world of mine. I realized that I really was the only one who could see through it all.

That may sound strange I know, but hand to the heavens it's true. It was like God had totally changed the playing field and the spiritual world was starting to take over. I knew in my heart what was happening and it hurt me deep inside.

Remember, I've understood this world differently since I was little.

Oh man, here comes that word again... F-E-A-R.

What was happening is this. God was becoming deeply upset at my husband and had decided to harden his heart and blind him from the truth. God was handing my husband over to his own very deadly desire, and the path he had chosen.

Sound cruel? No, it's not! It's not at all cruel. I truly believe that every Christian *needs* to be broken at some point in their life. It's the only way to truly go deeper with God.

Pruned if you do, and Pruned if you don't my friend!

What? That makes no sense to you? I get that, here let me explain it a little for you.

You see, my husband was about to understand the real meaning of:

1 Corinthians 10:13. Unfortunately, this is probably one of the most misused verses in the Bible.

It reads on most all feel good quotes:

And God is faithful; he will not let you be tempted beyond what you can bear....

Uh dude, that is NOT the whole verse! You need to read it ALL:

And God is faithful; he will not let you be tempted beyond what you can bear. But when you are tempted, he will also provide a way out so that you can endure it.

God will always provide a pathway through the valley, may not be easy, but you will be able to endure whatever is placed before you. Only one catch though, you have to accept it, and actually do the work to fix yourself!

You really got to understand something. God had given my husband *way more* than enough 'Get Outta Jail' free chances over the years. My husband could have taken the offer, got broken by choice, and gone deeper with God.

At each decision my husband made to decline Gods offer to repent and turn away, my husband got himself closer and closer to this moment coming in time. He could have turned away, and walked towards God many times. Only my husband had chosen to walk away from each offer God had given him.

However, in this marriage we are one, we're truly soul mates, even if one of us gets off the path. I know in my heart that we are meant to be together forever.

My husband had also forgotten that one little thing that my mom had said to him the first time she met him.

Remember what I told you that my mom said? *Do not ever doubt my daughter's connection to God.*

God was lovingly and strangely able to talk to me through the unique storyboard paintings that were forming in my little garage. I would sit still leaning over for hours, quietly painting in my garage. That was a miracle in itself since I can barely stand or walk long periods before getting severe back pain. But God had something to tell me and protected every part of me in it all. It was just comfortably safe in my garage.

One big problem for me though, God clearly told me of my role in it all. He told me that He needed me to, *Shut up and stay in the garage.*

I'm not kidding! He said it twice just to make sure I understood.

You would have to know me to understand why I really didn't want to follow that request. Oh ya, I am the type of person that is not scared of confrontation or face to face hard talks, even an all-out fight if done in truthful healthy anger.

On the one hand yes, I could absolutely understand Him telling me to do this.

On the other hand though, me keeping my mouth shut was, and probably still is, one of my biggest self-battle areas. So ya, you can probably imagine how hard it was for me to just Shut-Up.

I see my world falling apart around me, and I *now* know why, so I can stop it. So, why would God say to shut up and stay in the garage?

Well, I wanted to know that very thing and all God said back was, *Princess if you open your mouth you will ruin everything. Don't you trust me?*

I couldn't believe what He was telling me! So much in fact that, I convinced myself it was obviously the devil trying to fool me, and then I did exactly what God told me NOT to do. I went to my husband and begged him to stop and see what was going on.

At that moment my husband said, *I will stop it all tomorrow if you really want that.*

I thought YES! Ok, now we're getting somewhere!! But when I wanted to say, *Yes, stop it all!*

I could feel the words forming in my mouth...*YES, stop it all!*

Somewhere deep down inside me, my heart to God was true, and the words that came out were...*No, I trust you.*

At this point in time, no, I didn't trust my husband at all, but I honestly did trust God, and God knew I didn't want to mess up His plan. I was just hurting, mad and confused, but when the cards fell, I listened to Him and allowed His words to be spoken and not mine. I knew I had to go through whatever was coming.

There was no short cut to this victory and no way to jump this mountain. No, I was going to have to commit murder to win this one.

The next day came the kick in my gut that sent my emotions into a tailspin. My husband said to me, *You are acting crazy.*

Oh, hot chicky day dude!!! If there's anything you need to know about Midwest Country Girls, you do not EVER tell them they are acting crazy!!!

It's only acting crazy if it ain't true dude!

Unfortunately, this crazy world was not only real. I had a front-row seat to the crazyville horror show that I was watching with my very own eyes, yet being told that it wasn't what I saw it to be.

It was so upside down in my head that for one hot second I stopped and thought, *Maybe I am going bat crap crazy.*

Then God slapped me upside the head and said to get back to the garage.

Dude! It was all backwards in my home, and things would get very confusing when I was in the house. I couldn't seem to think straight from the funky sphere that was all around my husband.

After my husband said that gut kicking statement, I went into an emotional rage and stormed out to the garage.

With my tears flowing, I started creating: WARRIOR.

JUST AN ILLUSION

When I started "Just An Illusion" a few days later, I thought it was going to be a tribute to my grandma's painting from many years ago, and in a way it was, but it turned out to be much more than just that.

If you remember on the story pictures page, I mentioned that my grandma was a fantastic painter. She had actually made a painting for me when I was younger. I so treasured that painting.

Unfortunately, it got destroyed many years back when someone carelessly left it lying against a water heater that one day flooded, ruining my beautiful painting.

All I had left now were two pictures I had taken of the painting. I went upstairs to get one of the remaining pictures before heading out to the garage.

I could see the painting idea forming as I lay random pieces on the canvas, smiling to myself as all the little pieces seemed to just easily fall together.

I was really excited to make a painting in tribute to that beautiful painting my grandma had made for me so many years ago.

You don't understand I know, but if you would if you could have seen this painting my grandma made. This painting was not only unique, it also had a hidden thing about it. A hidden thing that very few people ever caught, which was precisely the point!

You had to look at it differently than what your eyes first viewed. You had to " *Tilt Your Head* "...when you viewed it.

Do you maybe remember that statement from earlier?
Yes? Ok, good.

It was about to be another amazing and very painful moment with God in my garage.

I was oddly happy this day, and I felt the mood lighten around me. I was chitty chatty with God in my garden, gathering the things I needed to make my new painting. It's funny that I remember it so clearly as I type these words. I guess because it was not just one enjoyable morning with God, but actually, the next few days were the same, which was really nice. It seemed as though things had finally calmed down for a minute.

A few days into the painting and the base could be seen. To be honest, for the first painting ever, I was quite pleased with how it was going.

And well, that should have been my first clue because then it happened, dangit.

A day or so later when I walked into my garage, it all felt different. The minute I opened the door, I felt a chill going down my back. I had that eerie feeling, and my stomach went into a tight knot.

I heard God clearly say, *Princess, the war is coming fast. I need you to listen to me very carefully.*

I froze like a deer in headlights! I didn't know what to do or say. *Did God just say a WAR was coming?*

I was suddenly so scared that I couldn't move. I couldn't even see any way to win what I thought was a massive battle in front of me, much less a WAR!

War? What? Why? How? Come on Lord, I'm past all that war stuff, right? I have been serving you faithfully for many years now.

I couldn't process the words I had just heard. Wasn't I smart enough by now to catch an issue at battle level? What could have slid by me that I missed a war forming?

I stood there for what felt like hours, and I'm not even really sure, maybe it was hours. All I remember is that I started painting, then my mind drifted off thinking about my grandma.

I miss her very much, my grandma and I were very close, and I was wishing she could have seen me standing here doing this.

I wish she was here Lord. She really would have loved to see this.

I drifted off thinking about one lovely summer day my grandma and I had together back on the ranch. Remembering back to a specific time when I was sitting with her in the painting room while she was telling me about swooshing, yes swooshing.

Trying to explain painting to me yet again, in another attempt to pull out a painter in me, which never took.

Remember the unicorn I painted? Ya, I'll just watch you paint grandma.

We would often sit in her paint room, I would watch her paint, and we would talk about whatever was of interest that day.

On this day while she was painting, she was swooshing, and she said, *You have to swoosh, stop, wipe and then swoosh again. Repeat this and don't forget to wipe or you'll mix the paints, and it will all bleed together. Swoosh, stop, wipe, swoosh, stop, wipe.*

Before I realized what was going on, I heard God's voice say...*Stop....*

I stopped, and when I did, it seemed as though I was suddenly back from my visit to grandmas in my head.

I finally snapped outta whatever of whatever. I stepped back to look at my painting, and that's when my jaw dropped open, for real!

I had just made the most perfect piece of color swooshing that I ever could have done!

I was standing there looking at it all smiles, when out of nowhere, I felt the words rising inside of me, *It's Just An Illusion.*

Remembering those words from my grandma about the painting she made for me so many years before, and now looking at my version, I *tilted my head* to look at it differently.

When I did, I suddenly felt that eerie feeling and my heart dropped. Needless to say, the ooohhh aaawww moment was over, reality was back, and God was trying to give me another weird puzzle piece.

The rest of the painting was nothing short of confusing. All I knew is that apparently a war was almost here. I wasn't allowed to do anything except, shut up and stay in the garage like I was told.

And that part about shutting up? Oh ya, that was becoming harder to do, with each passing day.

God kept repeating it to me all day, *It's just an illusion, what you are seeing is not real.*

I finally had enough and snapped back...*Ya, right! Just An illusion huh? Are you kidding me right now! I can see the REAL right in front of me! Where are you hanging out at anyway cuz I see it plain as day!! How can what I see in REAL LIFE be an illusion?*

I walked away from my garage that day feeling sick to my stomach and mumbling to myself, *Just an illusion? Ya right!*

CRY WITH ME

This spring morning was about to be anything but a lovely Saturday. For the past few days, I have been quiet, playing a game behind the scenes. Acting to my husband as if I was indeed, as dumb as he was hoping me to be.

Fine, I can play cat and mouse, you be mouse! Unfortunately, I had been down this road so many times in my life that it was like turning on autopilot.

This particular morning, I was sitting on the couch with my coffee while my husband had gone to shower and get ready to go to some event we had been invited to. An event I had no interest in going to, yet I also had no interest in staying home.

Anyway, the minute he stepped into the shower God said, *Are you ready?*
I said automatically, *Uuuhh Nope.*
He said very firmly, *It's time princess, I need you to look.*
I grabbed my husband's phone and opened it ...click ..click ..click.
I was just about to click one more time when God said, *Stop.*
I was already shaking so bad that I thought I would drop the phone. You see, I had already been on his phone and computer many times but found nothing.

I was about to click to the next area, and God said, *This is going to hurt you very much. Do you trust me?*
I said in the smallest voice I could find, *Yes, I trust you,* and then I clicked the button.
There is was! Everything, all of it, scrolling, scrolling, scrolling, then came my anger, pain, fear and finally rage was welling up inside me with each....scrolllllllll.
Needless to say, I snapped and the next few moments were like the standard cliché scene you'd expect. The door being dropkicked open, curtain ripped from its hinges, screaming in anger....
I found it all... DIVORCE!!!!

Well, let's just say, I launched the war into full speed motion! I continued to scream, demanding that my husband GET OUT! I couldn't breathe and I wanted my house empty, and fast! When my husband finally left, God *tried* to comfort and talk to me.

I was having NONE of that, and I yelled very loudly at Him, *God YOOOUUUUUU could have stopped all of this WEEKS ago!!! Why am I sitting here looking at my life shattered on the floor? YOU leave me alone! I mean it!*

A few hours later and my husband came back home.

Uh ya right, I don't think so dude! I was having none of that my friend! I stormed out the door to meet him in the driveway ready to say, *Go away and NEVER come back!*

But what fell out of my mouth was, *Go to your friend's house and go to church with them tomorrow!!!!*

Wait, what did I just say? Then looking at my husband's facial expression, he was just as shocked by my words.

I got so dadgum mad! I literally stomped my feet at both God and my husband.

GGGgggggrrrrrrring loudly through my teeth, I marched away waving my arms in the air saying, *Whatever Jerk! Come back tomorrow after church.*

When my husband left the house, I walked to my garden. That was when it all hit me; the overwhelming emotions of it all broke me right there. My knees went out from under me, and I hit the terrace ground. Utterly exhausted I laid there crying.

God was quiet the rest of the day, backing off and letting me breathe. I was so angry that anyone to approach me right now would get my rage snapped at them.

That night though, man I slept so well. I love it when angels wrap their wings around you in the middle of the storm, letting you sleep safely and protected.

Next morning is Sunday, and my husband is gone for church.
My non-church going husband that is!

Ya! That's why the comment I yelled at him the day before was so odd. He didn't even go to church!

But today, apparently God had his own plans, and I didn't care at this moment. I was numb, walking around in full zombie mode. I got my coffee and went out to the garden, where God was quietly waiting for me.

After a few moments I said softly, *I'm sorry for being mean yesterday, I didn't mean it.* I started crying, working my exit plan. I just wanted to leave this marriage. Set it all on fire and walk away.

After some time of God listening to my exit plan, He said something to me that was actually crazier than what I had just gone through.

He said, *I need you to love him through this.*

Well, uh ya, hot chicky day dude! My tears stopped in a hot second, and I gave my reply alright!

WHAT! Love him through this? Oh, I'll love him through this alright!

I'll love him through the front of my car, then cuz I Iooove him so very much, I will love him through the back of my car too!

Love him through this? Are you straight joking right now?

He then replied a little louder, *No! You WILL love him through this. When he comes home from church, you will walk up to him, you will hug him, and you will love him through this.*

I was in total shock and becoming very upset, very fast. I started spouting off my biblical rights, quoting verses that backed up my pain and the justice I wanted, claiming all the facts that I knew to be true.

And you know what? When I was done with my little rant, God also has something to say.

He lovingly yet very firmly reminded me, *Little girl don't you ever forget the times I've shown you the grace and mercy that you didn't deserve.*

Well, that shut me up.

Needless to say, I felt the emotions coming on and after I took myself down a harsh, quick stroll of memory lane and things way back when. I started crying and desperately apologizing again for all I did in my past.

Don't misunderstand me, God will never remind you of anything in your past, you're forgiven totally in His eyes. Your past sins are as far as the east is from the west.

However, He will remind you that at one or more times in your life, you were in dire need of His *Grace* and *Mercy*.

None of us are worthy or even deserve it, but yet, He gives it lovingly to every single one of us.

After some time of crying, and trying to get un-mad, I sincerely asked, *HOW? Lord, how can I possibly love him through this?*

Time stood still in my garden that day. I cried and cried telling God if this was true, and really what I had to do then I would do it. But! He had to do something for me.

I can't do this alone Lord, if you really need me to do this, then you MUST cry with me. Please, I'm begging you!! I NEED you to show me that this is really coming from you.

God wants your obedience, not your sacrifice. So, when my husband came home from church, I took all the strength I had left (literally) and walked right up to him, and I hugged him *with love*.

When I did, he fell hard into my arms weeping deeply, and crying beyond anything I had ever seen.

We sat down in two garden chairs facing each other, and there in the garden on a full blue sky day, my husband told me about church and how God made it directly at him. My husband's brokenness was apparent to see.

Then, the coolest thing happened. The sky was blue with no clouds in sight, and it started to lightly rain on both our arms, not much and not long, but totally long enough to make me laugh out loud, as I watched my loving Father crying with me!!!

The bizarre thing was when my husband laughed out loud at the same time and said to me, *Do you know why what just happened is so special?*

I said automatically, *Yes,* but then said, *Wait. Yes, I know why it's special to me, but you weren't here.*

What he told me next made me tilt my head. I mean, a full ear to shoulder touching, head tilt.

God absolutely cried with me!! Not only did He cry with me, He let my husband be part of his very first and far from last –

Christian Weird Moment!!

What did my husband tell me?

A story that reassured me in knowing; God was going to help me love my husband through this.

WHAT DO YOU DO NOW

Well, for me to go and say that the coming days were hard would be a vast understatement. I'm really sorry if you were hoping to read, *Oh God showed up, and all is ok now*. I wish I could say that believe you me, but the truth is that, the next days were nothing short of devastating.

All the lies and deceit lay before me in full light, and I just couldn't take it. I broke in the moment and began to spiral back to a dark and lonely place in my head, a place that if you are not careful will feel comfortable and all too familiar. I hadn't been to this place for many years, yet it felt like home to me in the moment.

Some of you will know exactly the place I talk about. If that is you, I am very sorry that you know this place. I don't wish that knowledge on anyone.

I tell it here so you can understand that you are not alone, as I said earlier, these sneaking and well-trained voices have tried to kill me since a very young age and just when I thought I could never be in their home again, here I was, and I felt myself disappearing.

I just couldn't believe it was true, I couldn't believe that I wasn't enough...again.

Then cue the skillful and familiar voices, A*gain you're not enough! Look at you, you're pathetic, never have been enough and never will be enough. You have no value. Do you even realize just how worthless you are?*

Sudden flashes of your childhood. Images you have begged God for years to erase from your memory, flashes that quickly become cruel and more personal.

I couldn't breathe from crying so hard. Realizing that yet again, here I am, alone and broken on a bathroom floor.

Then comes in that familiar calm voice, the one voice that seems to know how to talk to you better than all the others.

You can stop all the pain you know, you can take control and make it stop. It doesn't matter after because it will all be quiet, and you will finally be at peace.

I thought about everything in second flashes. I cried and then cried even harder, wanting to break the promise I had made in that tree when I was little.

Wanting to tell God, *You lied! It was NOT all worth it.*

I could feel my body wanting to crumble and just be done with it all. Feeling the intense pain that is starting to outweigh the soft words from God, quickly forgetting you ever even made a promise.

However! Unlike the times before!

I got mad! I mean, I got *Princess Warrior Daughter of God* mad!

Straight fed up with the devil mad!

I could clearly hear my Father's voice through all the screaming this time, and I knew exactly WHO was standing right beside me. I was no longer that lost scared little girl! I've been growing in God for many years now, and I know exactly who I am in Christ! And trust you me, there ain't no devil EVER going to get *MY* jeweled tiara that hangs in *MY* tree that has ALL its leaves!!! Uh, no way dude!

From deep inside me, I pulled in my breath as hard, and as deep as I could, and I *SCREAMED* at the top of my lungs, for as loud and as long as possible! When that breath was gone, I pulled it in again and screamed for as loud and long as the breath could go.

And with those two screams, I sent all the needed words, direct to my loving Father.

What? You think my scream was just a scream?

Oh no my friend, that's how I speak to God when I have no words. I guess you would say it's my language of speaking in tongues.

You see, many years ago, when I was going through a very hard time in my head. I didn't know how to explain my pain to God, the words just wouldn't form, but my pain at that moment was so deep, I just wanted to scream at the top of my lungs.

And God said, *Go ahead and scream*!

I didn't really understand what He meant and blew it off. Regaining my composure and pushing on in life.

Soon thereafter, I was driving over a railroad crossing, for some weird reason I suddenly thought about how loud trains were when passing by. Totally loud enough to muffle a scream!!

I immediately felt that urge to scream my lungs out again.

I drove to a place that I knew trains often passed by at, looking around to make sure no one was watching me..lol

And I screamed so loud and so hard, to not only one train, not even two trains. Nope, Dude I went through three scream trains!

I never felt so good in all my life! It was like HUGE weights had been lifted, and I knew in my heart, God totally understood my scream language just fine.

So yes, this time did go very different than the before life moments!

This time, I slowly pulled myself up off the floor. I was too tired to even think.

Stupid Devil!! Just shut up already. All you have is old news...

I wanted my bed, just pull the covers over my head and sleep it all away.

Is this really my new life?

Was the last thing I remembered thinking before I crashed into a deep sleep.

The next coming days I just wandered around in my garden, trying to figure out how to even start to heal from it all. My husband was trying to help, but when you're the cause of the pain, it's hard to be the one to comfort me.

After my husband understood what had just happened the day before, it caused him to go backwards and deal with more guilt that I had now placed on his shoulders, and to be honest, I was letting him go through it.

I was hurting, and inside I felt a little release in knowing that he was now feeling some of that deep pain like I had been going through for all these past months.

I knew in my heart that it wasn't healthy, but for the moment I just didn't care. I had shut down emotionally inside, and outside I was doing no more than walking around and going through the motions. I was the one now tucking myself away in my garage and garden, I didn't know what to do, and felt as though my heart was never going to mend.

You need to know that the next little bit is a gap fill of what happened before "Calling All Angels" officially started. I'll try to get through it as quickly as possible, but you really do need this information to understand how the second part of the painting series got started.

At a very young age, God gave me music to get me through difficult times. I would read the lyrics along, listening very carefully to the words being spoken. It's always been important to me because it is how God has always reached out to me in those darker times when I couldn't find the path. And this time in my life was the very definition of lost path.

My faith was strong, but my heart was damaged deeply, which can cause quite a battle inside of you. I turned up the music and faded away into my own imaginary non-painful world for a while. I just needed to breathe.

Some days later and still being lost in my head and emotions, I wanted out of the house. My husband offered to take me around to second-hand stores which I love so quickly accepted.

I feel something is significant, not only me to say right here, but for you to really understand.

My husband and I were not mean or cruel in words or actions towards each other through any of this. Of course, I went off in the beginning stages, but then I shut-up! We are very close and always will be.
I don't want anyone of you going off and judging him wrongfully! He's an amazing, loving man that lost his path, nothing more nothing less. He's human like we all are.

Anyway, we did go out and about that afternoon. I had a really lovely time, and it felt good to get away from the house and wander in the thrift stores. I came across little knick-knacks and enjoyed looking around at all the things that were helping to keep my mind off the situation.

Roaming through the store, I came across two little ceramic girl statues of a country style. One looked like it could hold a paintbrush, so of course, I quickly snatched it up to take a closer look.

It was a little broken and worn, but to me, I thought it was perfect. There was a second one also in a very similar style, but since I knew the one with the paintbrush was obviously for me, there was no reason to want the other one. Only, for some weird reason, I kept coming back to it. Eventually, I placed it in my basket and took it home with my other pieces.

When I got home later that day, I went to the garage and unpacked my items. I immediately placed the second statue back in a storage box, being sure I'd never need it anyway, and then went on with laying out my new found treasures from the day.

That next afternoon and I *really* wanted to go back out to the garage. I thought it was simply because I had these new items and wanted to play around, but whatever it was, it felt different. It didn't have a nervous feeling or anything to it, just a desire I felt inside.

I placed a new canvas on the table flat and started putting pieces on it. Some pieces of tree branches I had gathered from the garden, little sticks, and ripped lace strands. I started digging into old boxes, finding pieces here and there that seemed to be what I wanted. I came across a box of clay pieces that I had totally forgotten about. Smiling with excitement, I started to remove them and lay them out. It was all the little miniature pieces of my garden: my little fire pit, the birdhouse and feeder, and other tiny pieces that I had tried to sculpt out.

I put them onto the canvas and started giggling out loud a little as I realized that my garden and garage was slowly forming on the canvas. Quite pleased, I quickly wanted my new treasure of the country girl statue.

I was having fun playing around with all my little pieces, when...

Well, nothing! The desire to go further was gone just as quickly as it had arrived. *Hhmm that's odd*, I thought as fast as I forgot it.

Being late summer, I wanted to be in the sun doing nothing from my garden chair lounger while the days still allowed it. I walked away feeling a little weird, but again it wasn't fear or sadness, so I just let it be and went on about my day.

Soon enough though, I was back in the garage to do the last touches needed on the paintings you have read about so far. It was actually nice and quiet in the garage this particular morning, no screaming voices in my head.

I quickly offered my sincere thanks for shutting them up, if even for one moment. I decided to take advantage of the quiet moment in my head to ask God a very sincere question.

God, why do I have to be the one to pay the price for what he did? I'm over here shattered. He's forgiven and a new person in Christ. I really don't get how this is fair.

I was still so hurt from everything. I stopped what I was doing and went to the garden and cried, yet again. I asked God if He could please help me move forward. I felt so lonely and had no friends I could *really* talk to about any of it.

I waited and waited, but nothing. I didn't get any reply from God. So, with my feelings a little hurt, I left the garden and went back to the garage to finish the last things needed to complete the paintings.

Literally! The next day came a knock at my door

Uh ok, no one knocks on my door, ever. I answered, and it was my new neighbor that had recently moved in right next door. She had also lived many years in the States, so she spoke English! Even weirder is what she said next, *Would you like to have lunch with me sometime?*

I stood there for just a second, a little shocked at not being sure if I had heard her right, but it was true, and I did go to lunch with her.

A few days later at lunch together and we clicked nicely and were chatting along just fine. When somewhere between 'how the weather is' and 'what's your last name' I broke right there on the spot.

I then proceeded to flood this poor woman with my full story.

Oh ya, the full crazy version in all the weirdness and well, just everything.

After I was done and yes crying again. I realized what I had done, and instantly shame and embarrassment came over me.

Well, this woman without skipping a beat says, *Seems like you have needed that dump for a while....more wine?*

I laughed so hard, and it was nice, I mean really nice since I hadn't laughed in months.

Unfortunately, the mood quickly changed back to somber when she in return dumped her story. Sadly it was very similar to mine, maybe even worse since she was in the middle of a separation heading towards divorce. I hurt for her, like I hurt for my own self. I started thinking, *Is this becoming a common thing? What am I missing here Lord?*

After our good and much-needed dumping session, we talked the rest of the afternoon, and I thoroughly enjoyed the time with my new neighbor. Later at home in the garage, I thanked God for my new friend as I started bringing the paintings inside to hang throughout the house.

When I was coming inside, I started wondering and asked God, *Now what? The paintings are done. You told me what you needed to so we're done right?*

I felt like that was true, and honestly, I was ok with that. I felt drained and had God said to make another painting right now? Dude, I possibly could have flipped out from fear, thinking there was another deep dark secret hiding in the corner.

God knew I needed to have time to process it all.

Although, just a little bit of time is all I got before God turned my world upside down again!!!!

A few days later and I'm back looking at all the pieces lying on the canvas. Now cutting the worn lace angel wings that will wrap around the little garage structure I had, and placing next to it, the deer antler I had gotten from my grandmother's ranch many years before.

It was all coming along nicely and it was relaxing to finally make something that had no hidden secrets or painful truths to be figured out.

I messed around with it for some time longer enjoying the quiet. When I stopped, stood back and looked at it all. I remember loving it and thinking, *Cool, it's me alone in my garden with all my animals. I like that God, thank you.*

I still spent time here and there in the garage, little less in the garage now, and a little more with my husband.

My heart was *finally* not hurting at all hours of the day, and I even found breathing becoming a touch easier. I'm talking more with God, finally letting Him help me start to heal. Then maybe even eventually forgive and move on. It was working, slowly but surely it was working.

Although, it was still the featured movie that never stopped playing in the back of my mind. At this point, I was merely doing as I did back in the old days. I ignored the voices, best I could, and went on about my day.

Closing in on fall and by now, my husband and I are going down a very different path. He's still running full speed towards God, and I'm finally starting to enjoy seeing him be so happy. I'm watching as he is quickly understanding so many new things, and it's making my heart smile.

I'm still hurt, but it's my hurt to deal with, and I really want to do what God asked me to. I am not staying in this marriage to beat my husband over the head with what he did to me. No! That would mean I am *not* being obedient to what God asked of me.

I had to choose from what I had learned from Joyce: Complain and Remain or Praise and be Raised. I finally chose: *Praise and be Raised.*

You may not see it today, or even tomorrow, but I'm working on it.

Yes, of course, I was still hurt inside, and understandably so, it was all still so fresh. The voices were cruel to me and had been raging non-stop in my head for days now, but I had made a firm decision within myself.

I made a decision to stop giving that stupid devil, my mouth!

And I did just that! I kept my stinking mouth shut and dealt with my own internal pain. And now I'm screaming back at them in my head, day in and day out.

My husband had to go through whatever God took him through and the same for me. Oh sure! I wanted to tell my husband many things I *thought* and exactly how I *felt* about it all again and again, but would that be: *Loving him through it?* No, that would be making him pay over and over and over.

Whoever says being a Christian is easy, is not a real Christian!

I don't know if anyone famous ever said that, but I just said it right there and I mean it! It is not easy when you have rights on your side, and yet you must keep them to yourself.

I was fighting myself daily to just SHUT UP!

Then go ahead and add another area to the Christian plate: LOVE! Sincerely *love* him through it.

Dude! I was fighting daily battles inside. My flesh would say that it was all an act and my spirit would quickly remind me that you can't fake this stuff.

It all went back and forth like a never-ending tennis match, back and forth, back and forth. Cue the movie reply again, over and over and over. I couldn't seem to get the voices to stop, but I could keep from *sharing* them. I mean really, what good would it do? Sure, I could *sincerely* tell my husband what is still going on in my head, but that would only drag him down yet again and quite frankly, I now weirdly needed his crazy joy of God to keep my spirits up.

I know, crazy right?

Well, hang on tight, because this rodeo is far from being over.

Fall is coming in fast, and things are well on the mends in my home. Husband is loving me weirdly (which is a good thing) and doing all the needed things in his Christian life to grow up and be the man he wants to be for God and for me.

A short time later and I was standing in the garage just staring at the odd pieces that lay scattered on the canvas. I could feel myself starting to get anxious, now I was the one wanting to move forward on the painting.
But at each try... nothing, nodda.

Just a short time passes, and I was now walking out to my garden with a jacket on, watching the last of my flowers fade away. I sat down at the garden table and started off with my prayer, *Lord, I can't do this much longer. Please, I need something to help take my mind off this mess.*
Then I blurted out, *I need something to focus on God.*

Well, God heard me!
And apparently, the demons did too.

This morning was like all the others, yet again, a never-ending screaming match in my head. This particular morning though, I didn't yell back, I was either still tired or maybe not enough coffee yet, whatever the reason.
This time I said very calmly back to one of them, *Give it up already dude, I'm not going to say anything hurtful to my husband, so just drop it.*
Well, apparently that was the straw to break the demons back if you will. Because then, it YELLED back at me.
*Just open your *Bleeeep Bleeepp Bleeepp* mouth and say what I *Bleeeepppp*told you to say!*
Uh ok, that stopped me in my tracks. *What did you say? Did you just seriously demand me to say something 'for' you?*

I don't know why, but for some reason, it all hit me differently this one morning. I think I had finally had enough of the poor me pity party I had been showing up to *daily* for the last weeks.

The stupid voices invited me each day, and each day I kept showing up!

Well, when I went all calm and casual, apparently one demon flipped his lid. While, God probably said, Great! Finally! There you are girl!!

In an instant, a crazy row of light bulbs started going off, and I thought to myself, *That voice just demanded I say something out loud 'for' it, why?*

Ok, think girl, think... Let me walk this through.

Joyfully, I realized just how *insanely crazy mad* I was making them by *NOT* sharing my pitiful thoughts out loud to my husband.

OOOhhh snap!! It all just started clicking together like Tetris blocks in my head. *All of you are straight twisted up that my marriage still hasn't fallen apart!*

Ok Wait! If I can twist you up with something as simple as keeping my mouth shut, what if I go and flip other tables back around on you?

I could feel myself coming back to life inside, a sudden bud of life rose up inside me, and I thought, *Yes! I can do that, I mean come on man! I know these stupid demons as well as they know me! Ya, I like this plan, I'm sick of crying all the time! I want to make them cry for a change!*

Then I yelled out loud, *I'm going to start stalking demons!!!!*

And at that moment, the country girl woke back up inside me. I adjusted my jeweled tiara and got the heck outta that pity tree.

My mood suddenly changed after this, and my conversations with God became very different. Over coffee one morning, I popped off, *You know what God, I want all my stuff back! I want all the stuff those stupid demons have ever taken from me. How do I do that?*

Oh yes my friend, the country girl is coming back home, at a very fast pace.

The garage is getting cold now, but I have this area in the top left corner that needs only a few more touches. Finishing the last little gluing and wrapping the angel wings.

Yep, done for now.

I thought to myself as I set the painting aside, *I wonder what this one will end up being later.*

Oh wait, sorry, I probably just lost you didn't I?

Sorry about that. No you see, after my earlier demon stalking revelation? Oh ya, I spent the following weeks in the garage with God, just filling myself up with my new found strength.

I went full force on the painting, and the top pieces all fell into place, and now it was done.

Well, for the time being anyway, I locked the door to the garage and went back inside the house.

TIME JUMP TO CURRENT PRESENT:

As of this second, you're now in the present time with me. I've been stuck for the last two days in writing. I started to write the second half, and well, it just wasn't going right.

The words came to me ok enough, but they didn't flow like the first half. I stopped typing, knowing I clearly must have taken over at some point.

I read back what I had written so far this morning and ya, booooooring... It had ME written all over it. I tried to remove as much *me* writing as I could and well, it went all the way back up to here.

I knew it was pointless to try and save any of it, so I deleted it all and turned off the computer for a day.

You have to also understand, that right now in the present time while trying to write, things are funky in my house again.

Since our recent house guest arrived, the sphere is all outta whack. Sorry, I know it makes no sense to you now but it will soon enough, I promise. So, not knowing what to do now, I kicked back with the TV running in the background, and started talking to God, asking what was wrong. Why was it not going like the first half of my writing?

Through the evening I would get little nudges here and there in my heart telling me to, *Walk it through.*

I said, *Ok, walk what through?*

My problem with going forward was that, it's not really about the paintings anymore, and when I realized that, my words stopped, and I got stuck. So, I asked God exactly that, *How can I move forward? It's not really about the paintings anymore and the last three paintings kind of all fell into place, and then I was done.*

How can I explain all the crazy stuff that happened after? I mean, tell it and not bore them to sleep?

God *quickly* sent a few flashes from the area I am soon to write about and He gently said, *If you heard that story would you be bored?*

I laughed and said *No Sir! I would not be bored at all.*

He then explained it to me, and thank you Lord for not making me have to figure this one out!!

He said, *From here on out, it is all about 'moment choices' in time. Now it goes to being about you and your husband. You're stuck because you have to change your thinking and start writing as 'we' not 'me.' You see princess, as of now I'm about to show you that, you are no longer alone.*

I just smiled feeling Him hugging me and that night when my husband came home from his men's group meeting, I hugged him tight and said, *I'm not stuck anymore. I just had to walk it through is all.*

I woke up the next morning happy, really happy, because the sphere in the house is good. Well, it is for the next few days anyway, until my house guest returns.

Until then though, I have a feeling that the words will flow nicely, and that makes me smile. Because now, I can't wait to tell you what happened next!!!!

Before we start this next area, I need to give you a proper set-up. If I don't, you will completely miss the awesome punch-line I'll be delivering later.

Seriously dude, don't miss or skip this part. Ok, so from here on out my writing changes.

You see I'm FINALLY on the other side of the situation. The pain from before has faded.

I'm no longer in bondage within my head, and after my recent revelation, I got outta that pity tree, readjusted my tiara and never again did I go off and leave my sword lying at home! I went forward with the man I promised to love and cherish until death parts us. And happy ever after we will be!!!

You gotta get this!

Everything that happens from here on out is about 'Moment Choices.'

I mean a millisecond moment in time where your 'choice' or 'action' will have an immediate effect on the following moment in time.

Ok, you ready?

Welcome to what happened when LOVE was the choice I made.

TIME JUMP BACK TO THE STORY:

I'm reading a lot now in place of painting. I'm back on track and have decided I'm going to go back to doing what I am best at, broken teenagers! Yep, takes one to know one right? I already have a history of working with troubled teens, so yes, my mind is set, and I feel secure inside that it is the right step to take. I refuse to lose any more precious kids to nothing more than skillful, yet very predictable, voices inside their head.

Ok great, I have a plan!

Now what? Where can I find them? What do I do now?

I have a burning desire whelming up inside of me, but no clue what to do next. So I prayed, gave it to God, and went back to fixing my marriage, which is doing great by the way.

We have become closer than ever, and I'm easing down, slowly letting the walls that were built up fall away brick by brick.

Not long after this revelation of mine, and still on fire about trying to find a way to reach these troubled teens, we had a dinner meeting with a colleague and friend from out of town. We were at dinner talking about it, and all agreeing that teenagers these days went through so much more than when we were kids. I commented that here in the country we lived in, on average three teenagers per day commit suicide.

I also explained how years earlier I had already tried to get into areas locally to help, but I was blocked at every turn. I had fought hard enough and had gotten a foster daughter. She's all grown up now and doing well in her world.

But now so many years later and I was stuck as what to do next, and telling our friend that I was a little scared to step out and be bold because of the language barrier, stating that if that was not an issue I could do so much more.

Well, apparently my angel heard that last part of that sentence, and express delivered the information to God. Because what happened next is about to send my world into yet another tailspin!

The rest of the evening was lovely. My husband and I had earlier decided that I would drive home this evening. Which looking back now was a little odd in itself, because my husband always drives home, especially at night.

But this dinner evening was with my husband's friend, so I had said for them both to enjoy the company and wine, I would drive home this time.

MOMENT CHOICE:

Right before we left our friend to come back home, a situation came up that could have totally made us miss the next immediate moment!
A comment was made, and the past was quickly thrown right out there and directly in my face. I could have gotten mad and even rightfully mad, but I chose love in a millisecond and just dropped it.
Thankfully, the past had no real hold on me anymore, and I was able to shake it off and my husband also. Had we BOTH not chosen LOVE, the next moment would have been completely missed, because we would have been fighting and yelling in the car, not even LOOKING around us.

On the way home from dinner we passed over the railway crossing when suddenly my husband said, *Look there at that girl.*

I looked, but since I was driving and it was late in the night, I didn't see what he saw.

I said, *What is it?*

He replied, *That girl walking there so sad, didn't you see her?*

I quickly responded, *What do you mean sad? Like, oh poor girl walking late at night or you mean like BummerSheep turn around sad?*

He said in an instant, *BummerSheep sad, turnaround babe.*

I went around the next turn and drove back, as we crossed the railway again, there she was sitting next to the train tracks on a park bench. I pulled around the corner and parked the car. Looking nervously at my husband, I went to exit the car and said, *Ok, I'll be right back?*

It's late at night, cold and dark, but here I go walking up to a scared little girl sitting alone on a bench.

I started towards her and quickly talked up to God saying, *Ok God, whatever is whatever* and I sat down.

I looked at her and asked, *Are you ok?*

And in a small faint voice, I heard only one word from her, *No.*

I asked what was wrong and she said, *Everything in my life.*

I sat there for a few seconds as she looked only towards the ground, spinning in my head, *God what do I say!*

And well, this is what God so gracefully let fall out of my mouth, *Ok, uuumm I know this is usually how a bad movie starts, but I need you to trust me and come get in the car.*

She looked oddly at me, but for some reason, she just stood up and said, *Ok.*

I got her into the car and quickly made introductions between her and my husband and began driving home. She sat quiet in the back, not saying a word. We got home, and she sat down on the couch, hunched over and frightened. I could see anger and hurt was all over her.

My husband realized I needed the room alone with her, so he excused himself and went to bed.

The next couple of hours were intense, to say the least. She was in a bad spot in life, and in an even worse relationship. We were talking great, and I mean weird right?

God just happened to put a girl in the car that speaks perfect English?

Just a few short hours after me saying what I did at dinner? Coincidence? Ya, you're funny!

No, God was about to give me what I asked for, remember earlier when I asked, *Please give me something to focus on?*

Well, hot chicky day dude! Did He ever answer that request!

CALLING ALL ANGELS

The next couple of weeks were high stress of constant worry for me about this girl that God had brought suddenly into my life. She reminded me so much of me, which made me worry even more because I knew where she was.

She was fighting daily to not go away from this world, and each day that I didn't hear from her, I would freak out and worry thinking the worst: *Did she jump,? Did she take pills? Did that blade win? God help me, is she ok?*

I would run the worst-case scenarios through my head and worry, worry, worry.

Then finally, a text would come in from her, and I would calm down for a minute. Another weird thing is that she lived a very short distance from me, ya odd right?

However, her boyfriend was not allowing her to talk to me, that part actually worked out well for me, as him telling her no, made her pull even harder towards me. We soon found a secret place where we could meet up to talk, face to face.

I was now thinking about this girl every second of my day. My recent situation quickly took a backseat in my thinking which I appreciated very much! Although now, I had a very serious situation on my hands, Oh Lord! This girl!

Everything about her reminded me of myself way back when, her pain, her desire to go away from this cruel world, wanting a moment of peace inside her head.

Not only those things reminded me of myself, it was also her mannerisms, the way she walked and talked was also very similar to me. It was all becoming very familiar, and quite frankly, it was getting a little weird.

I never talked much, when she got around me, she talked and talked and talked. I listened and agreed, even if I didn't. I just nodded and listened to this sweet lost little girl dumping more of her life story at each meeting we had together.

One day she said something that not only made me stop in my tracks, it also made me laugh out loud. We met at our little sandwich shop, and before we left each other, I noticed that this time she was hanging onto the moment, and I could also feel that she wanted to say something.

So, I just asked her, *What is it?*

She looked at me. Wow, not towards the ground this time! No, this time she looked right into my eyes and said, *You know it's weird, but every time I am with you, the voices in my head go silent.*

I laughed out loud by accident, and looked right back at her with a big smile on my face and said, *Oh I understand that. You see, they know me, and when I come to meet you, I bring the big guns (my angel that is). So yes, I bet they do shut up when they see me coming. Don't worry sweetie, it's a good thing!*

I walked away laughing and smiling.

As I walked to the car, I popped off to the devil, *Soooo you're finally scared of ME are you, well that's reaaaaalllllll good to know cuz this little girl.... She's all mine you jerk!*

I prayed nonstop for words to help me not scare her away. God reminded me of my gift and said to start there. I smiled and said, *Ok, I can do that.* You see I have a special gift when it comes to introducing God and Jesus to people.

I will actually make you ask me about my God. It's true. Want to know how I do it? It's easy, don't tell them about God, yep you read right, I do not say ONE word about God.

Instead, I love them like a *normal* person, and I *show* them God in me by being an example, not a statement.

People like this young girl don't even know it at first, but the draw they have to *me* is not even *me*, it's the God I have *on* me and *in* me that they are feeling drawn to when they meet me.

The situation with this girl was very tricky, I know for a fact that if push too hard, she will pull away from me. But if I don't push hard enough, she will think I don't really care, so where is that line?

First things first, I need to build up her trust in me and get her strong enough to get out of this toxic relationship, and that's very hard in itself! You wouldn't, or even couldn't, understand this unless you have been in an abusive relationship, you can't just tell this girl GET OUT, she's not strong enough. This girl can barely survive the new day without killing herself, much less stand up to this bully and get away. So, pray and pray, and pray some more is all I could do. No longer is it my recent pain that I am thinking about, now it's this precious girl that keeps my mind spinning.

Not long at all, and we are texting every day, I mean many texting messages between us now, and I'm building her up, giving her strength.
Telling her that I'll be strong for us both until she can do it herself, just begging her to not give up.
Saying over and over... please trust me, please believe me, explaining to her that I can help with the voices in her head.

You understand why I can't talk about God yet, right?
She only knows what she's hearing, and she's hearing screaming voices, not Gods soft quiet voice in her head, she doesn't know God yet.
You can't tell her to hear a voice she doesn't *know*.
Baby steps my friend, baby steps.

It's becoming so bad right now, she can't seem to have one of her own real thoughts anymore. It's getting a little too close to the edge for her, and I can feel it.
I knew I had to push just a little harder.
God help me... I quickly prayed, typed the words and hit the send button.
I made my move and offered her a place in my home, telling her that she would be safe here. If she decided to leave she had a place to go, then I left it alone.

Late one night very soon after came a knock at my door, I opened it and there with bag in hand was this young girl. I jumped for joy (inside) and rushed her into the house.

Wanting to sing and dance, I held it in thinking to myself, *Careful crazy woman! She's fragile, don't show her that you're happy when she just walked out of a relationship.*

I held it in and sent up my thanks to the heavens and got her inside.

I find myself having a little bit of trouble going into this next part because it's not *my* story to tell. It's hers to tell you, and I would never throw her story all out there. Don't worry though, I happen to know that her story will be out there one day, just not today. So, for now, I'll write the *tiny glimpse* needed to go forward with mine.

The next days were difficult to put it mildly.

This poor girl was frozen in fear, the voices were screaming at her and not wanting her in my home, at all!

But what was strange is what happened each time we would walk to my garage. The closer we got to the garage, the more she relaxed, and I realized almost immediately what was happening.

Not telling her a thing, I tried to get her outside to the garage as much as possible.

I knew exactly what was going on, my strange little blessed garage was quickly becoming her safe place, just like it had been for me.

And talk she did! She had no idea, but I documented the whole thing from beginning to end, wanting to show her later just how much she had changed. I tried to do that with all my kids, telling them that keeping a journal is more for *you* than anything.

Anyway, in a short time this non-talking young girl (that everyone told me about) racked up over two hundred plus hours of talking, not *us* talking together, I mean all her. I would listen as she told it all.

Each time we came to the garage, she spilled more and more pain, hurt and fears, I listened and simply loved her through it all.

At night I would pray, but not from my bed though. Nope, I was on my living room floor with my mattress from upstairs, staying right next to her because she was afraid to sleep in the room alone. I had made her a promise that I had every intention of holding to.

I promised that I would never leave her alone, and never one step would she have to take by herself from here on out. I had every intention of holding to this promise, even though I had no clue of how.

She's been in my home for about a week now, and one morning I hear God telling me to, *Get ready.*

I quickly replied, *Get ready for what?*

Don't tell me God doesn't have a sense of humor, cuz I know for a fact He does!

Without skipping a beat, He replied. *Get ready to watch me, as you say it princess, Show up and Show off.*

I laughed and thanked God for making me laugh and joyfully replied, *Ok, yes please, I would really enjoy that.*

Then it happened, she was looking around my living room at the crosses and weird paintings, and she asked the question that made me laugh so hard I snorted at the same time. She popped off, *So are you some sort of Christian or something? I never hear you talk about God.*

Right there on the spot, my heart love tank was filled up. I said to God, *Oh Lord, aren't you the funny one.*

It was the special loving thing we do. God told me long ago
"You just love them normal, then I can get in and love them whole."

Meaning? You don't need to beat someone over the head with God, nor does every other word you say, need to include God this or Jesus that.

No, love them like a normal person, be their friend, listen to them and then let God come in and do His thing!

For the next few hours, we *lightly* talked about God, and I shared some things about my past to help level the field. She had told stuff about herself, and it was now my turn to let her know, she wasn't alone. We bonded over our pains and hurts, and quickly became close as we each started to see that our lives were similar in so many ways.

Honestly, I had no clue what to do next, so I did all I knew to do. I did to her what God did to me way back when.

I put Joyce Meyer on the TV. God brought Joyce into my life when I was in my late twenties. So, I decided I would go down the same path and see what happened.

I prayed sincerely, *Lord, this is all I know to do. Please take it and make it be enough for her to find you, let her finally be able to hear your soft voice through all the screaming. Please God, be with her now like you were there for me. In Jesus Name Amen.*

Oh my gosh, it was a little funny, well a lot funny actually. Joyce went off on a loving but very direct rant about getting out of your pity boat. This frightened little girl now big eyes looking at the TV, a little in shock that a preacher would speak out so direct.

However, I did watch her facial expression, and I saw that Joyce had grabbed her attention or rather that, Joyce had just quickly demanded it. We watched more that day, and I saw lights go off in her head. She asked very smart questions, and I could see this girl had more God in her than I had realized.

I continued to do the same to her as God had done to me back in my twenties. Joyce Meyer every-day / all-day, and then again the next day, all-day, and you know what? It was working for this sweet girl just as it had worked for me.

Certain messages were hitting points in her head, and she was starting to understand what was actually going on in her mind and that she was not alone.

It's all about planting seeds of truth my friend, you plant them where and when you can, and then you wait for God to make them grow.

Well, a few days later and I decided to switch it up and put on Craig Groeschel. He's my personal pastor and mentor since the late 90's, and I already knew the series to start with, "When the devil knocks."

It was a pretty new series at this time, and I had gotten very excited when I had first watched it. I even told my husband, *YES!! Craig is getting into the other side of it all. I'm so happy he's going in this direction*!!!

I loved the series and decided it was time to show it to...

You know what? Let's start calling her **PrincessT**!! I'm getting tired of writing *little frightened girl* or *scared young girl*.

The truth is, each day she was changing right before my eyes, turning into the princess I already knew she was. She just needed to be found is all.

Anyway, we watched the series and loved it, but then she made a very profound statement about something Craig had said, it was something along the lines of: *Oh, why are we going to talk about the devil? What I want you to understand is that, this is not a devil glorifying teaching, whatsoever.*

She looked at me, and with all sincerity she asked me, *Why not? Why don't you talk more about the devil and what he does? Maybe he should get more credit than you are all giving him".*

And with that, my heart dropped, from the mouths of children, right? And she was right. She needed to know more about the cruel voices in her head, and what to do with them. She needed an explanation of what was going on and how to start fighting back.

Who was this devil? What are his special powers and why was no one telling her more about him?

From there I changed my focus, and started telling her more about *me* and my past. I tried to help explain how I understood what the voices are and that she could learn to talk back to them and even control them.

Dude! Me and my big mouth! What am I doing!

With one try she wasn't having any more of that.

The day after I told her this and explained about talking back to the voices. Oh ya, she was alone in her room, late in the night, and she did it. She popped off at one of the voices, only then, they ALL turned on her and attacked her all night long with terrible dreams and ruthless memory flashes.

She was a wreck emotionally over the whole thing, and I quickly backed off knowing I was way out of my realm. I went out to the garage to talk to God. I was getting worried that I might be causing more confusion than good for PrincessT.

I asked God what to do, and all I got back was to keep doing exactly what I was doing. I hung out in the garage for a little longer and then I went back inside and did what I was told to.

I proceeded to shove as much God and truth in her as I could.

Holidays are now past and the New Year is here. I see PrincessT changing, but no longer in the forward movement. No, I see something else happening. She is starting to stall. She's not able to function, now getting stuck in daily routines. She's getting upset easily, and her voice is beginning to shut down, no more talking like before.

She's fighting inside over all the new truth and knowledge she has gotten so much of, so fast. She literally went on tilt and shut down.

I couldn't stop it, and I couldn't explain it, I could only sit back and watch. Soon after this started happening, she decided she wanted to go back home to her parents. This would have normally thrilled me, but it didn't and the reason why was that I knew in my heart, she was running away, not running home for the right reasons.

She was scared and didn't want to face the voices anymore right now. It was all too much. She wanted everything to stop for a minute. I felt sure I had broken her with too much weird information, and she now wanted as far away from me as possible.

It hurt way more than I expected it to when I watched her leave. I cried for the next coming days, watching my text messages, begging God to make her reach out to me.

Not one word. She was just....gone.

DON'T GET LOST

A week later and I still had no message from PrincessT. I had to shake it off and get back to my life and job, although she was never far from my thoughts. My husband was now able to comfort me over the current situation, and he's doing a fine job.

Unfortunately, the only information source I had about PrincessT was tainted, I didn't care though. I gladly played along. Anything to keep one foot in the door of her life, even if she didn't realize I was still in it.

I'm so crazy worried, I keep telling my husband, and he's trying to help by saying, *Don't worry, one day she will come back.*

I quickly finished the sentence for him and said, *HOME, One day she will come back...HOME!*

When she left and I realized that she was not coming back any time soon, I converted her bedroom into my new painting room for the rest of the winter. It was cozy and pleasant to be in her room. To me, it was still *her* room. I was only borrowing it until she came back *home*.

My heart was worried day and night about her. I was no longer thinking at all about the past situation, and really it didn't even have a hold on me anymore. I was trying to stay busy by moving forward on the canvas that had been lying here for so many months now.

I've now recently returned back to work together with my husband in our company. The company we had started together many years ago. Our paths had actually gotten separated quite some years back. I had always worked from home doing web design and other graphic style things. Over the years it had grown into a company from out of my house, and because so much of my focus was there, I left my husband to run our other company alone.

Hhmm maybe, just possibly that was *my* bad choice number one, way back when? See, if I were to be totally honest, I *knew* in the back of my mind that my husband couldn't do it alone. But I was more focused on what I wanted, and since at that time *my* company was funding *his* company. I felt it was more important to keep mine going full steam ahead.

Anyway, let's just say that my husband hadn't lost his path all by himself. It's a marriage, in which both of our choices matter and God was starting to show me some of my faults in it all.

Please understand me, I'm not trying to take away the blame in what my husband did. But you do need to understand something very important.

It's never just the one bad choice or the one bad plan from the one person in a marriage. It's a series of choices made by both of you, and whether you like it or not, those choices and decisions made by each of you, will eventually be added up, together!

God was now letting me see that maybe, just maybe, my husband wasn't the *only* one to hold some blame in all that had previously happened.

Anywho, perhaps that's all for another time, getting little deep there, don't want to lose anyone.

My painting was coming along nicely. I'm only doing a little in the evening or on the weekends. It's was nice and comfortable. I was healing well, and my marriage was good. I mean really good.

Coming back to work together with my husband was not only amazing, it was time together that we had missed. Remember, I told you we were always close, and we have always worked together, spent time together and then go home and spend more time together.

And now that our marriage was how it was supposed to be, it all starting changing. God is now my husband's first, and I'm second on his list, exactly how it supposed to be.

When it went to being a God centered marriage, then and only then could we start getting blessed in our marriage. Why all the sudden blessings? Because we were now walking together in God and He can *finally* bless us and *trust* us with more.

For many YEARS!!! I would tell my husband, *It just sucks that God can't bless us like I want.* My husband never understood what I meant, but I knew. I've always known that something was blocking us, something that I knew was God saying, *Sorry I just can't trust you with more yet.*

I would get so upset at times when my sales would go down or just suddenly stop. Saying to my husband, *I can't figure out what I've done for God to stop my sales. What could I be doing wrong?*

Well, duur thirteen years later, I know why! Even better than just me knowing why, we BOTH know why, and my husband has been walking a very different path.

He's getting closer and closer to God, and I see it. I not only see him listening and hearing God. My husband is now having talks with God.

Dude, I really couldn't be happier, talk about to the rim and overflowing!

For the next couple of months, God tucked my husband AND me away in work, and we were enjoying it. I'm finally feeling like the old me, but a better version, if that makes sense. We are getting closer every day by reading together and even praying together now. I have to admit that at first, it was odd. We were both a little nervous because we had never really prayed together, but we started, and now it would be odd if we didn't pray together!

Oh No! No No No...

That painting urge is coming on again, and on automatic instinct, I got scared. I twitched and thought, *Oh please not again*! I felt my knees get a little weak and I went into the upstairs paint room.

I quickly asked God, *What's the deal*!

All I felt was the strong need to pray, the need to pray for PrincessT. I'm praying in my head for her and also looking at the odd country scene now scattered all over the canvas.

I have the top corner done, and we all know it's me alone in my garden with my animals. But all these new little pieces that I've been laying on it randomly over time are not making any sense, and now it's getting all cluttered. Not wanting to deal with the mess, I decided to go in another direction. Ya, I know right! When will I ever learn...

Let's just quickly jump through my dumb plan, shall we?
Weeellll, I decided that I wanted my husband more in my painting world. Yep, hubby's never done artsy stuff, and now his wife wants him to paint, so he does.

I gave him a painting that had been hanging out in the garage called "Don't Get Lost." I never finished it and never felt the need to either. Honestly, I loved it just as is. It reminded me to, Keep It Simple, and well, Don't Get Lost.

Buuuut, I wanted my husband to paint with me! So much in fact, that I convinced myself the "Don't Get Lost" painting must actually be his; easily explaining why it had never been finished.

Fully convincing myself of that, I gave it to him and he, well he, he messed it all up, is what he did!

Watching in horror and trying not to freak out, as it took all I had in me to not snatch it back before it's beyond repair.

But I just smiled and said, *Oh that's pretty.*

Very soon after though, I did take it back!!!

My husband was thrilled to give it back, as he never wanted to do it in the first place, he just did it to make me happy.

I grabbed my painting and headed to the paint room to start fixing what my husband messed up, lol.

Ok, so now I'm back on track and no longer trying to make anyone play in the painting room with me.

Thankfully Pastor Craig says mistakes are called: wisdom.

Dude, by now I must be one *very* wise woman.

Life is going very nice at this point in time. I'm enjoying work, and my home is in good balance. More doors and blessings are happening behind the scenes, and you can feel Gods love and presence in our marriage and in our home.

I felt like I was watching what happened *because* I chose LOVE.
I really did *Put On Love*! I really did it!
I chose the path that did, take me straight into the fire.
And now, I was on the other side looking at the sum of my recent decisions now being added up.
God was doing so much so fast, and I knew that my feeling inside was right. Something was coming, I could feel it.

In my paint room finishing the last touches for the "Don't' Get Lost" painting. It wasn't done, I could tell that, but I just had this idea for a BIGGER one, I *really* wanted to get started on.
Suddenly, a text popped up on my phone from a family member of PrincessT. Everything STOP!
I quickly read it, and they were asking if we wanted to come and have coffee, stating that she wanted to see me.
I quickly replied, *YES!!!*
And with a bounce in my step, I turned up the music and went back to the last touches before setting aside the 'Don't Get Lost' painting and wondering to myself, *What are you up to now God?*

The day is here, and I'm like a little kid, *I get to see her today*!! I kept saying all morning with a smile from ear to ear.
We arrive later that morning to the house of PrincessT. I'm all happy, walking with a spring in my step, right up until the front door opened.
Dude! When we walked in the house, I suddenly got all twisted up in my gut. I looked over at my husband, and he had the same look.
Oh snap, I know this feeling. We were now in a heavy environment. You could feel the heavy pushing in on your chest with each step further into the house. We sat down, and I wasn't sure what to do, so I sat straight up in the beautiful home that surrounded me. It was all pretty and shiny with eye-catching displays placed all around the room.

PrincessT came in and sat beside me. I was fidgety and doing what I always do when I feel uncomfortable.

I forgot one thing though, this little princess sitting next to me knows me so very well, like this bad habit I do when I get in situations like this.

I was sitting there, drilling my fingernail into the side of my other finger. Don't know why I do it. I've done it as long as I can remember.

Anyway, within a hot minute, PrincessT leans over to me and says, *Don't do that.*

I said, *Don't do what?*

She looked at my finger, then she looked back at me and said, *That right there, don't do that. It's ok, just calm down.*

And in that second, I knew that this was far from over between her and me. This princess was working it out slowly in her head, God was getting in and doing His thing. We stayed a short time longer then returned home. The sphere was not comforting or inviting to stay in, but I needed to be there. Because at least now, I knew the environment that she was staying in, which greatly helps in knowing *how* to pray for her until I can get her back home.

Dangit! Days later and still no text! I was hoping that the coffee visit would start her texting me again, but nothing. I tried to keep the worry away, as much as I could, but this girl was etched in my head.

I went back to the painting room and again laid the canvas with random pieces down on the table. I was about to start moving pieces around when I remembered the second country girl statue, which strangely I now had a strong need to find.

Wait, what did I do with that? *Oh come on! Lord that was months ago, it's got to be way in the bottom of a box somewhere, I'm never going to be able to find that. Oh look, that's funny, here is it is right here, you're so funny God.*

I hope you're starting to see how much He wants to talk to us and help us to find many lost things? If you ever listen for just a minute, He might make you crack a smile. Listen a little longer, and He might even make you laugh out loud!

Suddenly, over the next coming days, the odd little pieces starting to slowly make sense and I realized, *Yep! Another odd storyboard is forming.*

Only this time, I was getting excited.

Why? Because from the minute I got the second country girl statue out, I *KNEW* it had something to do with PrincessT, and I wanted to know what it all meant.

The spring air is fading, and summer warmth is coming in. I'm back out in the garden being lazy, doing things that make me smile. I'm growing in God and getting a nice flow going in my marriage, family, kids, and home.

At this point though, the painting is now becoming a bit of an addiction. I know it means something about PrincessT, but can't figure it all out. All I know is that each time I start on it, I also start praying for her in my head.

Ok, few days pass and I'm getting really antsy, talking to God as always, except today I'm like a little kid on a sugar rush.

PPLEZZZZZ tell me what this all means. Plez Plez Plez give me another hint, it has been days, pleezzzzz.

It had almost become a game between us by now.

I was having fun, and God was also teasing me at times and making me laugh out loud or giggle in joy throughout the day in random public places.

For instance, one day I was in the store getting my groceries, and out of nowhere, the gambling chips made sense.

She made a bet on you, you made a bet on her, and I made a bet on you both.

I smiled and said, *Oh that's so awesome. I love that!*

I left the store smiling and went home to go further on the painting and to enjoy the garden.

A few weeks later and it's finished, I've now figured out what it all means, and it's absolutely one of my favorites.

Looking at it and reading the story all across the canvas, I now understand that if I just stay in the background, I will indeed get a harvest from what I had sown. God made it clear that now, I had to hand PrincessT over to Him and wait.

Nope, I didn't get the answers I *wanted*, but the painting sure made my heart smile in knowing I did do ok, and now it was God's turn to get in there and love her whole.

My husband is being amazing and supporting me in everything, better than that, he's becoming pretty weird himself!

I placed the "Calling All Angels" painting on display in my living room. This way I can see it every day, and know that God will keep His word and bring her back home when He's ready.

End of summer is creeping in and I finally received a one-sentence text from PrincessT.

Sorry, I lost my faith for a minute, but I found it back, talk soon.

I jumped up and down and told my husband, *She's ok, I didn't break her, she's ok!!!!*

Smiling from ear to ear and giggling joyfully, I went out to the garden and thanked God with ALL my heart!

LOVE WILL ALWAYS WIN

I couldn't be happier right now, dancing in the paint room and thanking God. *She's ok! Thank you, thank you so much!*

Wait, she said found her faith?!?!

I thought it all through, like I do everything and while I was making the color background for the canvas, my mind wandered in other directions, *Did she miss me at all God? Did she find You? Do you think she even knows how she helped save my marriage?!?*

I swiped the canvas trying to copy the lady I watched do it on TV, really still just lost in my thoughts about her text.

Ok, this isn't working, focus girl! I went back to painting and trying to remember how that lady did it. She made it look so easy on TV! She just went swipe, and then swipe, and then Taa Daa she was done.

However, mine was going a little less smooth, but still ending up way better than I expected which let me know I was doing what I was supposed to be doing at that moment. Otherwise, it would look more like that sad attempt at a unicorn way back when with grandma.

A few days later and I came bouncing into the living room, announcing loudly to my husband, *PrincessT is coming over today*!!!!

My husband went to the train station later that morning and brought her back home for the afternoon.

It was like she had never left, we started talking just as before. I offered up my sincere thanks to God and thoroughly enjoyed her being home, even if it was just for an afternoon.

Yes!! Thank you Lord!! She's back to texting me at least once a day and I'm replying with short replies, trying to hold in my excitement and not overflow her message box.

She has come back to visit a few times here and there, and I can tell she's doing ok enough, but something isn't quite right. I could feel it but didn't know how to get her to tell me. All I knew was for right now, I was by no means going to push! I just wanted her in my life and wasn't about to chance pushing too hard, for fear she would pull away from me.

The next weeks, I took every chance I could get to be with her, asking God to clear a path and He did.

One day when I went to have lunch with her and her girlfriend, at the last minute, the place PrincessT worked at, called and said she didn't need to come in that evening.

I knew this was my chance, knowing for sure that her girlfriend could stay the night too. See, I knew having her friend with her would help to make it low stress for PrincessT, and next morning they head back together.

They both wanted to come and stay, so of course, I was NOT missing this chance and immediately said, *Yes.*

I often say and firmly believe:
"If it's easy, it's not enough!"

This sleepover was not convenient for me by any means, my husband and I had an early flight the next morning, but I called my husband and said I what I was doing. He of course, couldn't say no to my smiling happy voice over the phone.

Enjoying the warmth of summer, we decided to have a BBQ that evening with the girls in the garden. It was perfect, and the girls laughed and giggled as young girls should. I was thinking to myself how happy I was!!! I didn't think it could get any better than this moment in life right now, seeing my girl sitting right here next to me, smiling and happy. *God is good, God is so Goooooood.*

Oh snap! I was up late with the girls having fun, and geesh, it's early now. My husband, as I said earlier, has been getting really Christian weird and one totally weird moment was this.

Months before he had come across a Hillsong Conference commercial that stated the conference would be coming close to where we lived, well close, it was a short flight away, but totally doable.

He looked at me with big kid like eyes and said, *Want to go?*

I could tell what he really wanted to say was, *Plez can we go, plez plez plez.*

I smiled outside, but inside, I had another moment choice to make.

MOMENT CHOICE:
I did smile, and I did say yes. Then I sent up a quick prayer, *God you know I don't want anything to do with this! I seriously have to go to one of those, over the top, meeting events with tens of thousands of people?!? UUuggg ok fine. I'll go, and I will go gladly, but please let me get something out of it too, please!*

And with that fast sincere LOVE choice, off to Hillsong we went.

There Is More!!!! That was the Hillsong theme line: "There Is More."

I sure didn't feel that way at the time though! I didn't want to be there at all. I don't like crowds or loud noises, and I get uncomfortable being crammed into stadium chairs next to strangers, and blah blah blah.

But I came for my husband and I was *sincerely* here for him. I was not dragging my feet all day, complaining about every little thing.

No, I was really *there* for him and God.

Little did I know, but I was about to get a big fat lesson myself!

We're finally at the apartment, landed a couple hours ago. I'm getting settled in while my husband goes to get the tickets at the stadium across the street.

You have to understand that he has been planning this trip for months. He wanted it all to be perfect, perfect for me that is.

He booked the apartment months ago so that we could be as close as possible to the stadium, and he did great, we are right across the street.

Did I mention that he was doing it all for me? Yes, he's awesome like that, and he planned it all this way for me because I'm sick.

There I said it. I never talk about it, and after this, you will probably never hear me bring it up again but yes, I am sick. I live with multiple chronic diseases, so any sort of travel or long distance journeys are challenging for me, so all this planning he did was for me.

He's always cared for me perfectly, it's not like this is a new thing he's doing. He's really amazing and has always cared beautifully for me in all we have been through over the years with my health.

So anyway, he planned it all down to the last detail, and I knew he wanted this time for us to grow back together.

And truly we are back stronger and even closer than we were before. I know that sounds so cliché, but it's true, and now we are walking the weird path together.

He's catching things out in the real world that helps me to see and believe that yes, he really does start to see and understand the bigger picture. He really understands how to look at the world now. Not how he used to see it, but for how it *really* is.

And he's getting it! Not only that, but he's getting it *fast* and I'm loving it!!

I mean FOR REAL!!!

FINALLY, I'm no longer WEIRD alone.

Seriously dude, can you imagine? I have been weird like this since I was five years old! No one has ever been on this weird level with me, ever!

It's been incredibly lonely living in a world that you see entirely different than others around you. I have known and understood about that *in between* world since I was little, and I also understood its special powers to jack up our level in this world.

Now come on! Don't go thinking, *Yep here she goes...off her rocker.*

I'm not saying that I walk around all day and see angels or demons flying through the air. I don't go casting demons outta doorknobs or stupid stuff like that.

No!! I mean the *atmosphere* around you. That feeling you get out of nowhere when you meet someone or that quick feeling that something isn't right. Oh my favorite one, when that strange knot suddenly twists in your gut and the hair on the back of your neck stands up.

That's the stuff I'm talking about.

I've been sensitive to that for so long, and it's really effortless to see me (*if you know how to see me)* in different situations, how my body language will quickly change.

Well, weird enough. My husband is feeling that stuff on me now, and it's really weird to me, because now when I get twisted up, he is suddenly turning to me at the same time asking if I'm ok. The second or third time he did it I said, *Dude, you're getting weird! Thank You!!*

Ok, husband is back from getting our tickets from across the street.

Uuhh where are the tickets? He sighed out deeply as he started with his story, poor guy, he was so upset. Turns out that we were not only, not across the street from the stadium, but we were actually on the wrong side of town, and at the wrong stadium all together!

Oh ya, all his months of planning and trying to do every detail right have officially flown right out the window.

He was explaining that we now had to take multiple subway trams to get there, not only that, but we would need to leave an hour earlier to get there in time, and last but not least, it was all going to be travel during rush hour.

My poor sweet husband was getting more devastated by each word of his story. Knowing the travel he was about to put me through, and frankly, I was about to cry knowing I was going to have to do it.

MOMENT CHOICE:
I could have easily joined in and helped my husband think it's a disaster. Saying it was all now pointless and ruined, and quickly believing that I would never be able to handle the travel... blah blah blah

Instead, I popped off, *It's ok. It's obviously for a reason, we just need to keep our eyes open for why it all happened this way.*

I lifted him back up, stating that God would never bring me here and then ask me to suffer in pain.

As long as I did what I was told to do, and be happy doing it, I knew God would wrap His love around my body, and I would be just fine.

God had this trip covered, and Oh Lord did He ever!!!

Ok, quick change of plans. I need to make a sandwich to eat on the tram, my body is not feeling so grand, and I'm trying to pray as fast and as hard as possible before we get in the metal sardine tram bullet.

I don't like subway trams, they freak me out.

Anyway, baby steps get on a tram, baby steps get on a tram, you are in the tram …

I quickly searched for a seat and saw one open next to a homeless lady so I sat down next to her and then I realized, she won't look at me.

I thought to myself, *I'm so sorry that others looked at you wrong so long, so long that now you won't even look at me, I see you, I promise I do.*

In that second I saw her turn towards me, just barely and only enough to catch my face for a second, so I smiled quickly to her and with that smile she stopped. She didn't get up to move away from me, she almost did, but my smile eased her back down.

Next stop is coming and I have this sandwich in my bag. I ask God, *should I?* I never know in these situations, I've been next to many homeless people over the years, and I never want to offend anyone, so I always pray and ask first.

I love homeless people, I love them very much, and you will always find me looking for them when we go to new towns.

Anyway, the next stop arrives and people shuffle in and out. Off we go again, and now a lady has sat down on the other side of the homeless woman, in one quick move the homeless lady was up from her seat and now standing by the exit door.

I shook it off and thought that she must be getting off at the next stop, *Ok, then maybe I wasn't to give her the sandwich.*

I see my husband looking at me now from where he is standing in the tram, the homeless lady is standing right next to him. I'm looking at him signaling to my sandwich, trying to convey, if he thought I should give it to her. He didn't understand my meaning, and I didn't think it mattered anymore since I thought the next stop was when she would exit.

Oh wait, the tram door closed, and she's still standing there. Then I felt my stomach twist. My husband wasn't moving or making any attempt to talk to her, so I did what I do best.

I stood up and walked over to her and asked, *Would you like this sandwich?* She popped off back, *I would like some money!* So I popped off back, *Well ya, I'd like a new car, but at the end of the day, you still gotta eat.*

And with that simple mess of words, she turned towards me, and we started talking like old friends that had not seen each other in years.

Wow, her eyes are crazy beautiful! If you looked at her like most people, you would never see it, but when I look at people, I look directly into their eyes, and hers were stunning! She told her life story in less than a few minutes as we shot through the tunnels, saying that she was originally from Ireland, I didn't catch her name, I think it started with a J, what did she say?

I couldn't hear now because the doors were closing at her stop and I'm literally hanging out the tram door still talking when she says, *You can always find me at Kings Cross.*

Doors to the tram shut, and off we go to the conference. While we are talking about what had just happened, we both caught it out of the corner of our eye, a sign that read... ANGEL... then quickly it passed again... ANGEL... then it was gone.

We ignored the sign that had just flashed by, and went on talking about my new friend. I'm happy inside and now I'm even looking forward to the conference evening.

I also know what I want to do the next coming day!!! I want to go to Kings Cross and find my new friend.

Ok, so here we are in a crowd of over 20,000 people waiting to get in. I don't mind though, I have my new friend on my mind and feel good about our trip so far. We get inside and find our group area, soon after comes a fantastic speaker and the music was awesome, God put me in my place about the 'over the top' thing.

When you have thousands and thousands of people singing to God, it's a very moving moment.

So in an instant, I'm here for more than just my husband.

Oh look, *There Really Is More.* Huh, whooda thunk it?

We talked about the service all the way back, and really the tram ride for me ended up being no big deal at all.

Next day we walked around a bit and enjoyed the time together before we head off to Kings Cross to search for my new friend.

We arrived at Kings Cross, and when we came out from the tram station area, my husband asked, *How do we find her?*

Laughing and walking along I said, *You find her like this.*

I'm having fun right now, and I'm about to show my husband just how weird I really am. You see, being around and interacting with homeless people is my thing! I'm in my comfort zone here. How is that? Ya, that's a whole other story my friend.

Anyway, we come out of the tram station, and I look for the closest police officer or security person.

Oh there's a male officer right there, *Come on babe,* I said and started walking towards the officer. I'm a country girl yes, but I do so love to make people *tilt their head* at me. You know that head tilt I'm talking about, the one a dog does when it hears a strange noise.

Ya, that head tilt! I love making people do that towards me.

So anyway, I walk right up to him and say with a big smile, *Where do the homeless people hang at around here?*

Oh, there's that head tilt...gotta love it.

I then continued and explained that I was looking for someone and they said we could always find them here, so I assumed there was an area, and there was. He pointed us to up around the building to a sitting area.

While we walked that way, I explained to my husband that we needed to find the homeless guy or woman that stands out.

82

Meaning, they have the most stuff, they are in the best area spot to watch everyone, and they will be the most outspoken.

We come around the building, and I quickly search the people, bags, places, location and yep, there's the guy I am looking for right over there.

My husband is really just following me at this point, as we are way outside his comfort zone. He's never really done stuff like this, and I can feel him watching me, but right now I'm on a mission. I want to find my friend and find out more about her.

We talked to the main guy, and I quickly gave a very detailed outlay of the woman, and he said, *Sorry I would know if that were anyone here, but it's not.* And with that sentence, my bubble of excitement popped.

What does he mean she's not here? I can feel her here, I looked desperately at my husband, and he could see it on my face. We started walking around looking for her. I just thought maybe the guy didn't want us to find her, he could have thought we were not sincere. Whatever the reason, I felt he was wrong.

I kept telling my husband, *I know what I'm feeling is her. What am I missing? I feel her all around me, where is she!!*

Then God starts in on me saying *LOOK*, and I would look, but see nothing, again a few minutes later He said again, *LOOK!*

I am looking! I don't see her! I looked up the stairs, down the side alley...NOTHING.

I'm starting to get upset and crying to my husband telling him that God keeps saying to LOOK!!

I am looking! But I can't find her, and now I felt all twisted up inside.

Not being able to find her, we eventually walked back to our tram, knowing that we needed to get going to the conference. I'm crying and trying not to cry because there are people all around me in the tram, and it's getting busy too, with each stop, more people crammed into the tram.

I'm still spinning in my head and I can also start to feel that God is upset with me. I have that urge inside, like I need to apologize for something, but for what? What did I just miss?

Dude, it's getting cramped in this tram, I can't move and as I looked up to my husband, I could feel it coming.

You have GOT to be KIDDING ME! A panic attack! Seriously!

I haven't had a panic attack in years, and never have I had one around my husband. I'm praying like a crazy person, begging God to make it stop.

I can't breathe, and now my husband realizes I'm freaking out. I'm grabbing the cross on my necklace, and my husband knows that this is what I do when I get scared.

He's quickly leaning into me trying to hold me and make it all ok, but it's too late, I feel it coming on strong. Crying hard and trying to catch my breath.

I have to get out of here, God please stop the tram!!!!!

Doors finally open and I bust out almost hitting the wall ahead of me, I hit the ground shaking, and my husband is trying to understand what is happening so he can calm me down.

A lady passing offered me her water, and I snatched it saying a fast thank you while trying to stop shaking. After a minute or five of sitting there, my sweet dork of a husband pops off, *So, to many people in the tram huh?*

I looked at him and popped off back, *Ya think?*

Now, with both of us smiling, he pulled me up and held me close until the next sardine tram showed up.

Oh man, I thought we'd never get here, I told my husband, then stating that I needed a drink before we go in. I had to calm down outside in the open breeze before being able to willingly walk into a building and join 20,000+ people inside.

We talked briefly about what happened, although it wasn't the time to go into depth about it, as the service would be starting soon.

Earlier when we were at Kings Cross, the homeless guy we talked to said that later in the evening was a better time to find someone, explaining that during the day most of the homeless people would be sleeping.

Before we went in for the service, I asked my husband if we could go back to Kings Cross after so I could try to find her.

He smiled and said, *Of course we can*, and with that instantly calming me down we went in for the evening service.

Music is amazing! I'm feeling the soft flow of His presence.

I said to Him, *It's incredible to be here God. I'm sorry for whatever I missed today.*

I did not get the reply back that I was expecting though.

He said, *Why didn't you find me today?*

I didn't understand that at all and said back, *I didn't know I was looking for you?*

Again he said, *Why didn't you find me today?*

I could feel my heart starting to hurt, but I had no idea what He was talking about, so again, I went back to watching the service.

Soon after He said, *I was right there, why didn't you look?*

Now I was getting upset and said, *Ok God, what is the deal? I was looking! I tried to find her all afternoon!*

Then He said more firmly to me, *Why were you looking for her? I was right there.*

Ok, whatever Lord, you're being weird, and again I went back to watching the service.

Then sudden flashes from God, that directly dropped this stupid little country girl to her knees.

In a place of over 20,000 people, I hit the ground crying on the spot!

He then said in a very stern voice, *I was right there, why didn't you LOOK!*

A flashed image hit my mind. The young teenage girl that was sleeping at the top of the stairs by the tram station exit, Oh man! That forgotten girl I walked right past. Not once but two times.

Then the man by the service bar, the man that was looking right at me. I was too busy to look back to him, I just passed him by looking towards my own interest.

Then remembering the older lady that was sleeping in the sun and my heart dropped. I could have sat next to her and given some shade by simply blocking the sun with my body.

I hadn't *LOOKED* at all that day, and when I didn't think I could feel any worse, the ANGEL sign my husband and I had both seen fell into my head.

ANGEL!!! *Oh, Snap! That was YOU in the tram*! Now rethinking the words she had said to me from outside the tram, *You can always find me at Kings Cross.*

I cried even harder. I hadn't even caught it, of course, I could always find HIM at Kings Cross. I know this! God deeply loves the ones that others have thrown away. I know this for a fact! God had given me ALL the signs I needed, and I still didn't catch it!

After the service, we waited at the side lounge area until the other 20,000+ people crammed themselves into the subway lines.

While we waited, I told my husband what happened in the service, and he also shared revelations he had gotten as well.

He lit up when he realized that he had just seen his very first ANGEL!

I smiled really big because I had forgotten, this is all new to my husband, and it really was cool watching it all now through his eyes.

After some time and we were off, heading again to Kings Cross, back to look properly this time. When we got there, we searched for the nearest McDonald's. I ordered ten cheeseburgers and the girl gave an odd look, tilted her head at me, and then went to gather my items. We got the burgers and headed back across the street.

I explained that when you walk by, don't intrude on their personal area, it's a protective thing for them. Just smile and ask if they would like a warm burger, then read their body language, you will quickly see if they want your conversation or just the food.

So far so good, everyone is friendly and accepting of us, as we passed by one younger girl, we asked if she would like a burger. She was busy in her bags but quickly took the burger. Then just as fast, she turned back to what she was doing, we just smiled and walked on.

Next was a lady we both saw at the same time, I thought to myself as soon as I looked at her, *Wait she stands out here. She has nice clothes and even jewelry? What is she doing out here on the street?*

I offered her a burger, and she gladly accepted. I noticed that she was still looking at me, so I asked if we could maybe sit down and eat a burger with her, stating that I was starting to get a little hungry myself. She agreed to our company, and we sat down.

Is that a cross around her neck? So I asked, *Are you Christian?* She said, *Yes* and started to talk about verses and stuff that I didn't see coming, she knew her Bible better than me?!?! *What is she doing out here?*

Then I saw her walking up behind my husband, the girl from before that grabbed the burger and turned away, she was now walking over to us.

Slowly she approached us saying, *I'm so sorry, I didn't mean to be rude. I just wanted to thank you, I do appreciate the burger.* We asked her to sit down and join us. And with that, we met our first two new friends which we found by LOOKING with the proper view.

This young girl that had now joined us looked to be in her late twenties and let me tell you, she was a little, little thing! I mean nothing but skin and bones.

She started talking along nicely, and chatted for quite some time. Before leaving, we agreed to meet with the young girl that next day afternoon before our church conference.

My husband and I were talking and sharing so many things that evening after we got back to the apartment. It was really cool for me and actually a whole new world was starting to open for me.

You have to understand, I have never had anyone in my life to share this weirdness with, much less someone quickly becoming as weird as me!

That next afternoon before we met up with her, I had first done what I do best, be a bonus mom.

We had gone earlier that morning to the local store and bought for her: blankets, sweaters, socks, shoes...etc.

It's what I do and I'll never stop.

When we met up and got settled at the park, I gave her the items I had bought. I have a nonchalant way I give things like this. I always go through it fast, and then casually lay it to the side, not trying to bring attention to what was there. I start talking about something and direct it all back to conversation as if the items presented never happened.

You never want to make someone feel wrong or bad about the things you give them. Set it aside and go on being a normal loving person to them.

It should be what you do to show love, not something you do to be noticed.

We spent the afternoon sitting in the park talking and again making plans to meet up later that night after the service.

The service was amazing and we thoroughly enjoyed the speakers and worship music. After the service we went back to Kings Cross and walked to the restaurant that we had agreed to meet at. We didn't see her there yet, so realizing that she must be running a little late we decided to wait outside in the fresh air.

A short time later we saw her crossing the street. She was quickly walking towards the restaurant. She hadn't spotted us across the street yet, but we could see that she was frantically looking in the windows at the restaurant. When she couldn't find us, you could see that she was starting to panic, thinking that she had missed us altogether.

My husband yelled out to her, and she heard his voice *immediately*, and when she spotted him, she started walking quickly over to us.

Only this time, she wasn't coming to me, she went straight to my husband and buried her head into his chest, hugging him so tightly. I watched my husband melt right there on the spot as he wrapped his arms around her. Oh Snap! God had just given my husband his own Princess.

We now call her PrincessJay by the way. It was a lovely evening, talking for some time longer, then hugging each other and again making plans to meet the next afternoon before the conference.

Last day of the conference and we really couldn't be more thankful to God for all He has let us experience these last days. Again we met PrincessJay for lunch and we, of course, made arrangements to meet up with her after the service.

Hillsong Theme remember it? .... **There Is More**...

Well on the high of the last night, knowing the service was right at me! I have been announced, and I know it!! I got bold and offered to others in our church group to go with us to Kings Cross.

I mean the service was just about this very thing, right? Ok, I can do that!! But unfortunately, I got no takers, *really*?

A little thrown and a lot shocked, I just shrugged, *Whatever dudes*.

We're outta here and off we went to go back and hang with PrincessJay before going home the next morning.

This time she was there early waiting for us to arrive. It was a bittersweet meeting as we had to tell her we were leaving the next morning. We explained that this was only goodbye for now, although she didn't take it well at all. She was sitting in between us crying at hearing us tell her that we would be leaving.

I gave her all our information of emails and phone numbers to make sure she knew we are not leaving her, we just had to go home. She promised to call or email, saying that she had a friend who would let her send us a text and let us know she was ok. With our hearts heavy we walked away from PrincessJay.

Next day or two being back home, and still on the conference high, making plans to move forward with my area for troubled teens. My husband is now really motivated to help, and I'm enjoying it. It has been tough for me to try and get it all going, so having help was very much welcomed.

Ok, a week now and no word from PrincessJay, says my husband!

Ya, that wasn't me saying it, that was my husband, and I could feel his pain. We had been worried about her since our return home. Both of us thought for sure we would have heard from her in a few days, but here we were a week later and not one word from her.

I was getting really worried, but my husband was straight trippen over it all. He couldn't stop thinking about her and worrying like the great dad that he is. God had let this little girl get deep into his heart, my husband was becoming just as weird as me, and I loved it!

How weird has he gotten you ask?

Oh, please let me tell you just how weird he's gotten.

At this point in time, it's justa few short weeks until we celebrate my husband's birthday and one day, he lets me know what he wants for his birthday.

I want us to fly back over to where PrincessJay is and make sure she's ok.

I looked at him, and honestly, I had never loved him more in my life than right at that very second.

I quickly agreed, and off he went smiling to make the apartment and flight arrangements.

In between going back, I have been talking daily again with my PrincessT. She was about to go back to school!! I was so excited for her, knowing this time she could pull it off.

I lifted her up as high as I could, telling her how proud I was of her, asking her about the courses and wanting to know if she was happy.

The last question stumped her for a minute, I knew it! She wasn't happy!!! She was being that smiley to your face but still hurting inside fake happy.

I changed the subject by telling her about PrincessJay and all that had happened on our trip. We had a nice talk and made plans for her to come over after we got back from the second trip to PrincessJay.

I was missing her so much. I just wanted PrincessT to be HAPPY.

A short time later and we are in the apartment rental, back to the city where PrincessJay lives. Needing to wait until it got later in the night before we could go look for PrincessJay, we decided to roam around the city and enjoy the day. Walking around I soon figured out that we were staying only two blocks away from Kings Cross. I giggled to myself thinking, *My husband really got us close to her.*

Later that afternoon we went behind the apartments looking for a grocery store to get some items for the night.

There we met Daniel, a young guy sitting on his blanket with a few of his belongings beside him.

As we walked up, I did as I always do and looked directly in his eyes, smiled and said, *Hi.*

He said *Hi* right back and looked straight into my eyes.

There's my queue, I said to myself smiling, and asked if he wanted anything from in the store. He said he would like some orange juice and gummy bears. I smiled and went inside the store, leaving my husband there to talk with him.

When I came back outside, they were talking right along. I enjoyed seeing this very much. I appreciated my husband so much for going all in on learning how to SEE people, not just noticing them.

Daniel was a sweet guy, and we said our goodbyes for now, sure we would see him the next day when we went for groceries.

Dude, you scared the bejeebers outta me!!!....
I didn't even get the time to say...

PRINCESSJAY!!!!! My husband yells from right behind me, in my ear, on a busy side street, late at night!

I jumped dude, I mean I JUMPED! Thought I done been shot jumped!

I was in the middle of saying, *Dude, you scared the bejeebers outta me*, when my husband passes by me yelling, *There she is! Do you see her?!?...* PRINCESSJAY!!!

I'm trying to catch up saying, *Yes I see her! Be careful!*

We were alongside a busy and crazy corner road!!

And when he yelled the second time, PrincessJay snapped her head up and looked around.

When she saw my husband standing there, she stopped instantly, and when she realized it *really* was him, she ran to him! Meaning she also ran right into the busy street!

Now I am screaming, *Be Careful! Watch out*, but she's trucking it straight to him.

And just as before, she went straight to my husband and buried her head in his chest crying and asking what we were doing there, he hugged her tight for a moment.

After she calmed down, and me too, we went to the local restaurant and started talking. We desperately wanted to know why we hadn't heard from her. And after hearing what happened, both our hearts dropped. She's a little thing, just skin and bones remember? Well, that's not a good combination when you are on the streets.

As she's talking though, my husband is starting to realize, she's not being sincere, and he knows she isn't *really* trying to get off the streets.

I pretty much knew that already; I just didn't really care. I only wanted to make sure she was ok.

Long story short, it was true. She wasn't trying to get off the streets at all.

And that's when I realized just how weird my husband was becoming!

Ok, so now he has a twist in his gut at the restaurant table. He knows something isn't right, and I'm looking at him, trying to understand what he's thinking, but I didn't catch what he did, and now he keeps looking at me funny.

Anyway, remember when I said that people don't even realize it, but it's the God *on* me and *in* me that they are drawn to when they meet me?

Well, that same thing is true in the opposite, some people can't stand me. They decide that immediately or spin out later. Either way, they feel uncomfortable around me and pull away.

Except that now I am watching that change be felt by PrincessJay from my husband, the instant his feelings *changed*. Her attitude *changed* too.

Soon after when we were walking down the street to take PrincessJay to her location, she said something under her breath, *If you guys have something to say, just say it.*

I played it off and said, *What did you say?*

She repeated it, *If you have something to say, just say it.*

My husband and I both kept walking along with her, acting like we had no idea what she was talking about.

When we left her shortly thereafter, it was said to meet the next day by the grocery store behind the apartment where we were staying.

Long story short, she never showed up.

Ya dangit! The stupid voices tricked her, by making her feel shame and guilt. She didn't mean to hurt us, and she sure didn't mean to try and play us, it's just in her nature. She's lived many years now on the streets, and it's really the only way of life that she knows. We were not upset, and to be honest, she really didn't even actually play us, it was only those cruel lying voices in her head that wouldn't let her come be with us.

Waiting at the grocery store the next day, we got to talking to Daniel again, now our buddy as we've seen him quite often passing by the last days. He's a really caring guy and knowing his story, you just gotta love him!

I walked inside to get orange juice and gummy bears while my husband talked with him. We waited some time longer and knowing that PrincessJay wasn't coming, we walked back towards Kings Cross.

We knew it was a long shot trying to find her, being midday now it was likely we wouldn't find her. We looked and looked but no PrincessJay, with nothing more we could do, we returned home.

I still to this current day don't know if she's ok, but I can tell you that as I'm writing this, we will actually be going back in just a few months and we will be going to where she is and make sure she is doing ok.

Why? Why would we bother?
Because you may not be able to save everyone, but you can *always* love them through it. Sure, she may never get off the street, it is what it is, and unfortunately, many people I know simply don't ever do the work to fix their life.

My husband and I can only do, what we do very well together now as a couple, we will love her normal.

Remember what I said earlier: *If it's easy, it's not enough!*

We will go and let her know that we are right here and that we haven't gone anywhere. While we are there, we will go and get the things she needs and do what we can for her. Then we will hug her and tell her that we love her and we will come back home.

You have to learn to just love them normal dude!

Back home and summer is fading, we are getting back into the swing of work and getting our kids sent back to college and stuff. I often talk with PrincessT by text, and we are getting that bond going again, and I can feel her pulling back to me.

A short time later and I come sliding into the room, playing my air guitar singing, *My favorite band is coming*!!!

I've been stalking the band schedule for months now, just waiting for their agenda to come out for my area.

I do not like concerts much, because I don't like many people around me, *but* with that being said, if I will get to hear: Front Porch Trained.

I will get there! However it is needed!

Why?
Oh, I'm so glad you asked!

I married my husband in 2004.
My husband married me *back* in 2017.

Here, let me explain that statement a little for you. After everything that happened between my husband and I back in 2017, we had later gone away for a weekend to reconnect.

And that weekend getaway, ended up being a NEW wedding weekend for us. It was the best weekend I've ever had in my entire life!

My husband and I have a favorite place we often went to on the weekends, and finally, I was ready to go back and stay a weekend there. This particular weekend there was a music festival going and many bands were from the USA.

We enjoyed the day together, listening to music and walking around the city, then coming back later to see who was playing on stage.

It was all just lovely, and I couldn't have been happier. My mood was perfect, I was in love all over again with my husband and well, life was just good!

In the afternoon we had found an amazing ring maker, and of course, one ring caught my eye.

I was in love with it before I even got close up to it.

It had leaves folded around each side, little flowers etched along the band, and well, it said *My Garden* all over it.

My eyes went big, and then of course, it fit perfectly.

My husband smiled and said it was my new wedding ring.

I smiled and gladly accepted that.

Later we went back to the music festival, and after some time sitting there enjoying the different bands. I hear a sound! A sound like HOME!!

With the slide slide slide of a familiar sound, I snapped my head around to the stage.

He has a slide guitar!! I yelled to my husband as I'm now walking quickly towards the stage. Ya, me the person that doesn't like crowds is now the person that is pushing their way to the front, and when I do....

They started playing: Front Porch Trained!!!

Oh my gosh dude, I came unglued!!! I was hearing the words and laughed out loud yelling, *How did you know! I'm front porched trained too*!

I'm jumping around like a pogo stick, and my husband is watching me and smiling. It was perfect! It was absolutely the most amazing weekend ever! And now we even have a wedding song..lol Front Porch Trained!

Do you know who else music is really important to? My PrincessT.

She and I had often turned up Front porch Trained in the house yelling the words and dancing around being stupid.

But her and me, our song is: We Deserve A Happy Ending!

The upcoming concert is going to be a celebration for all three of us. After all we have been through over the last year? Dude, I couldn't wait for a celebration!!

Make sure PrincessT is there, and we're all good, I told my husband.

I'm about to make my move! See by now, I know she's not happy, home life is as it was before, tearing her down and telling her all the things she will soon fail at, yet again. I'm fed up and really want her home.

She's pulling back to me, and she's realizing that *blood* doesn't make a family, *love* makes a family.

I knew she had to go back home so God could help her to look at things, *with her head tilted*.

I couldn't make her see it, my husband couldn't make her see it, only God could, and He was doing just that!

I knew, that I knew, this concert was going to be the thing that brought her home! I had all the plans made: husband-CHECK, my girlfriend from next door-CHECK, PrincessT-CHECK.

Yes, I just know it's all going to be perfect.

The concert day is finally here, and my stomach is in knots, God has been chatting all morning and I'm so happy right now that I can't stop looking at the clock.

Tonight, was going to be our night, a celebration of the year we all three had now put behind us.

She was different, I was different, my husband was different, we were all getting weird, and I was lovin every minute of it.

Of course, God had set the scene perfectly!

Not many people and not really crowded. I couldn't believe it, I looked at my husband and almost started crying. I was feeling my heart grow every second with joy.

Then, we had a perfect place up front, the perfection made by God just for me set my tears flowing. The music started and my heart jumped out of my chest, I had no words, no way to say how thankful I was to God.

I felt like my heart would explode if I couldn't tell God how happy I felt.

And then God said it, *Go ahead and scream princess.*

So, I did, all night long! My apologies to the band, but dude I totally needed those screams!

The night was all I could have hoped for, and I could finally scream out LOVE!!!

Oh man, for the first time ever, my screams were *love* words. It felt amazing, I screamed so loud to my loving Father up above, saying all the things I had no words for, but screaming out to Him with so much honor and so much love for all He had done for me.

Midway through playing, the crazy cool chick that plays the washboard leaned over to me (wearing my jeweled purple tiara) and she asks, *Is it your birthday?*

I said, *Nope, I'm a real live princess!*

With that, she went back to playing, now smiling oddly at me.

Yep, there goes that head tilt, gotta love it.

I watched a lovely older couple in front, right by us, as they danced and laughed together, enjoying the music in their own little world. He twirled her around, smiling and singing, they were just adorable.

Then the older man put out his hand towards me, asking if I wanted to dance. I quickly responded by grabbing his hand, and he started twirling me around like a little kid.

Twirling – twirling- twirling and singing to myself....
Ollie Ollie, I'm Frreeeeee!!!

When the concert was over, we spoke shortly to the band members and took a few pictures, then after getting a T-shirt, off we went all together back HOME!

We laughed and talked for a short bit after we got back, PrincessT and me taking pictures of her hands where the band had signed them for her. She was laughing and giggling like a young girl should, and with that making my heart smile, we ended the perfect evening.

Next day she stayed for the morning, and then went back to her parents. *I want her home*, I told my husband after she left.

He hugged me tight as we both stood there looking at the painting, I had made with the two country girl statues.

The painting that turned out to not be about me at all, it was all about her, and she didn't even know it!

A few days later and a lot of texting back and forth, she finally told me she can't take it anymore. She really wants to do well in school, and this time she's totally motivated, but she said, *If I stay here, I will fail.*

God help!! Here's my chance, do I say it? With a gentle reassuring feeling in my heart, I knew it was ok to say it now.

I typed the words... *You know that you always have a place here. You can come back anytime you want.* I didn't know if I should have said it almost immediately after I hit the send button, but I needed her to know that she wasn't stuck anywhere.

About two weeks later, and guess who's coming HOME!!!!! I quickly started to get things ready for her return. Paints are going into another side bedroom, moving things and getting her bed back in place, clearing out the boxes and replacing them with pictures and things to make it feel cozy.

I wanted her to *want* to stay this time, and I was really nervous that she would be here for a short time like before only to then leave again.

Lord, please let her be able to feel at home this time.

Yes, she's home! She's doing good in school, little issues here and there, but man she's working through them way faster than before. We are talking all the time, and slowly I'm helping her ease down on her moods.

Because we all know that at age nineteen, everyone is wrong except you, of course...lol

So, I'm changing my stance and no longer talking to her like a parent, now I'm popping off with her like a sister. Letting her get upset and spill what she thought or felt about something, then I would jokingly pop off something back, but more of a comment that made her, well, tilt her head a little.

See, I wasn't coming out and telling her that the way she viewed things was wrong.

No way! You don't do that; you gently love them into the direction you want them to go. She's a smart girl, she is getting my odd comments and not really funny joke returns, she knows me, and I know her.

I'm slowly getting her to ease down and see that, *the whole world is not out to get her.* I can only softly show her that she's simply looking at it wrong. She needed to, *Tilt Her Head* a little more is all.

I'm also getting up with her each morning. Uuuuhh ya, not only am I getting up early, I'm getting up at 5:15am in the morning! Oh ya, me and my BIG mouth!

I am NOT a morning person, guess who else ain't a morning person? You guessed it, my not so little PrincessT.

I told her, *If you do it, I'll do it with you!* Yep, famous last words.

Oh Lord have mercy!!! The first few weeks were a lot just to get that girl outta her bed at 5:15am!

Good thing I'm a little brat when I want to be..hehehe. My husband had a great idea, and I ran with it and made it a reality. We were like little kids giggling and laughing the whole time we were setting it up.

You know those remote front doorbell things? The one that you can scroll through five to ten terrible front door chimes, oh yes we did.

My husband remembered one day that we still had that thing in the house somewhere. I started laughing and said I knew where it was.

We put the batteries in and then went through the sounds to decide which one was the loudest and most annoying.

Oh my goodness, there was a loud one that kind of sounded like the theme song to the old western show Bonanza.

We laughed and went upstairs to PrincessT's bedroom. We decided to hide it on the bookshelf right above her head.

And then we waited for the next morning at 5:15am.

I hear her alarm go off and then, nothing, she wasn't getting up again this morning. This time I'm not upset though, I'm quietly laughing, rolling over to see my husband smiling too.

I cracked up and said, *It was your great plan, you wanna hit the button.*

He laughed and said, *Yes please.*

DUN DEE DE DUN DUN....DUN DUN DUN DE DI TI!!!! Off goes the doorbell cowboy theme song.... PrincessT is now screaming and jumping out of her bed.

As for us, we were laughing our butts off in the other room and I yelled out, *Good morning grasshopper, GET OUTTA BED!!!*

Well, let's just say from that moment on, it was a lot easier to get her out of that bed in the morning. I'm sure it also helped that I kept moving the doorbell thing around in her room, so she couldn't find it and remove the batteries.

I walked away each morning laughing to myself, *I only have to be smarter than the object I'm trying to operate.*

A few weeks down the road and PrincessT's first set of grades will be coming in, she's rocking it at school, and we are watching her quickly busting out of the box others had put her in over the years.

She's beaming God, and the girl has now sidestepped over ten years of hard road that I had gone down, by choosing to *believe* in Him and let Him work inside her.

She had not only accepted the weird people we are, she was quickly gaining ground and about to catch up to us.

I'm getting really nervous for the first set of grades to come in. I really want her to do well so that I can send it to her family and get them to just back off! On the other hand, I don't care at ALL about her grades. I'm just so crazy proud of her, she has officially made it through her first semester of school!

She not only didn't bomb out, she's getting really interested in her study, and I see her watching shows on TV in her area of study, and she's watching documentaries on her laptop. I mean who wouldn't be proud?

I do want her grades to be good, but not for me, for her. I want her confidence to start building, and start seeing herself the way my husband and I see her.

Oh gosh, I'm so nervous!! The first grade of exams is coming in today. She's about to be home and I don't want to be overly excited.

What if it wasn't good? I heard somewhere in the back of my mind.

I quickly snapped back, *Dude! Of course they're good grades! You jerk!*

In she comes and I try to be as calm as I could and ask, *Sssooo how was your day?* She said, *Good* and walked to the teapot.

I know this girl, little grasshopper of mine, and she's now messing with me. I finally said, *Ok already tell me, what is the grade?*

She smiled and said she got a perfect 10.

I flipped out, a perfect 10!!! My girl got a perfect 10 on her first exam. *Thank you Lord, You are AWESOMESAUCE!!* The following grades were just as excellent, and she leveled out at a fantastic top grade.

From there not only did she bust out of that stupid box. She set the box on fire and walked away!!! I was now looking at a proper front porch trained, God loving, beautiful young lady!

The next coming weeks get a little unusual though. I know right, there's more? Uuuhhh yepper!

TIME JUMP TO CURRENT PRESENT:
Ok, by now you know I'm weird, right? Well, I have been like this forever and a day, and back in 2012 I went on a search. I wanted to find a place to donate to, a place that cared for orphans somewhere in a forgotten place. I don't give to the big places, sorry I just don't. I know it doesn't *ALL* go direct and I wanted that personal and direct contact. So, I prayed and gave it to God.

About a year later on social media, I saw some pictures from my girlfriend back home. She had sent some clothes and things to a guy in Uganda. Curious, I went and viewed the pictures and read her comments. I clicked the button and went to this guy's media page, and soon after that, I messaged him. We hit it off and talked more about what he did and wanted to do.

And Loooonnnngggg story short.
After this guy from Uganda had traveled to our home a few times, we became family, and I became really interested in what he and his wife were doing.

I jumped in and started working with them. It was going great, and we were doing projects together, and building it all up quite well. I had adopted a fifteen year old boy named Ronald. By 'adopted' I mean that I fully funded him there in Uganda at the home of our newly made friends. At this time they had about 6 children living with them in their home, as well as a child of their own.

My husband back then was really only letting me do and be however I wanted, his heart wasn't in it back then like it is now.

Anyway, in 2015 it came time for the need to visit Uganda and see things there in person. We wanted to build a water well, but you need to be there to see the situation in a whole before being able to move forward.

Ok, you remember I earlier stated that I was sick? Ok, so I tried to get my doctor to let me go, and I got a big fat NO. I really did understand why though, just two years before I had a major attack on my system and almost died. I was well on the mends by this time, but having no immune system at this point means that going to a place like Uganda right now was not going to happen.

I'm really bull-headed when I want something though, and since I couldn't go, I was going to make my husband go for me. And I do mean *making* him go because he didn't want to go, at all. Saying that he was too busy, and work was moving fast and blah blah blah.

Eventually, I wore him down, and he agreed to go.

It ended up being a fantastic trip for my husband in Uganda, and a lot of information had been gathered for the water project.

And my husband when he got back?

Oh, you could see he was not the same man. Not only was he softer when he returned, but he also informed me that we had now adopted two more and possibly a third child there in Uganda.

I laughed and knew it was the right thing for him to have gone.

Oh sure, I could have ignored the doctor and gone, but I didn't *need* it. I love those kids from here, just as I would love them in person, it's just my nature. My husband however, really *needed* them to touch him and grab his heart in person.

He was still seeing them as people WAY OVER there.

No!! They are not WAY OVER there.

They are *RIGHT THERE*!

He got that now.

TIME JUMP BACK TO STORY:

Now already late in the summer, and I walk into our living room and announce to my husband, *I want to go to Uganda.*

Not only have I decided that I want to go, but I want to go that coming Christmas for the upcoming holiday party. I'm feeling terrific and have been doing exceptionally well for the last couple of years, I can feel it, this is my year to go.

Honestly, you never know what the future holds, and I've learned to never pass up an opportunity for travel and making memories.

My husband is in agreement with me, and now I just have to reach out to my doctor.

And he finally said music to my ears, *If you're going to do it, do it now.*

And with that, I got really excited. I'm finally going to get to hug my bonus kids in person! I really wasn't sure if I would ever be healthy enough to make this trip, but I was, and I was now planning the trip together with my husband.

I also knew who else I wanted to take with us. Yep, you guessed it! I wanted PrincessT with me on this trip.

I just knew in my heart that, the last pieces she needed to fully understand God and His love, was there in Uganda.

I talked it over with my husband, and we both agreed that it was the perfect gift for our upcoming anniversary. We asked for the help of our family over in Uganda to make a video present for PrincessT.

In a couple of weeks, we will be celebrating our one year anniversary of meeting PrincessT.

Remember way back when, on that dark and lonely park bench?

Ya Buddy, it's only been one year, and just look at what God has done in this girl.

We had dinner plans set and the day is here, our official one year together. We are all three in the house getting ready, joking around with each other, and just enjoying the time together.

I'm so excited to give her the video announcement we have for her gift. My husband and I both were teasing her all day. Having fun in making her crazy of wanting to know what her present was.

Later at dinner, we gave her the video present. She was in shock and had to watch the video again. Looking at us from across the dinner table, and you see the big crocodile tears coming.
No way! You guys are going to make me cry, stop it.
Dinner was awesome, and we quickly started talking and making plans for our trip to Uganda.

We only have a few weeks before we go, and trying to book flights and get everything arranged was a little hectic, but it's all done, and we are going to Uganda!!!

Dude! I do not even know *how* to put into words, of what all happened in Uganda, not sure I even can really. So again, let's do a tiny glimpse, cuz man, the Uganda trip is a long storybook all on its own.
Who knows though, maybe this whole writing thing goes further, and I'll get the chance to tell you all about it someday.

Anywho, we get there, and it's the scene you'd expect. Everyone has come to meet us at the airport.
I see my bonus son, now almost twenty years old, is pushing his way to me, he's set to be the first one to hug me and he is.
I'm now crying and hugging him tight, he's crying and hugging me tighter. I felt my heart growing with every hug I received. I waited so very long to hug my bonus kids!!!

We first went to the hotel and got some rest. It was a really long flight and need to get settled in, knowing we would have hectic days to come.

Outside by the hotel pool area the next morning, we were all happy to no longer be at home in the cold days of winter, now feeling the warm summer heat and enjoying the clear blue skies.

Oh ya, this warm summer weather will do me just fine.

Breakfast is over and we are on our way to the home of our friends where all the kids are waiting for us.

I'm wondering in the back of my mind, *How is my daughter going to react to all this.*

Oh ya, by the way, PrincessT, she's all mine now! We have officially gone to being *mom and daughter.*

She's my treasure! I will *never* ever throw her away, and she knows it! Blood does not make a family! LOVE makes a family and my awesome daughter, she really understands that now.

So anyway, *How is my daughter going to react to all this?*

It's a sincere question to have since she's never experienced something like this before. Is it going to overwhelm her and she pull away? Is it going to be too much to fast?

I wanted her to have fun and be the child she was never allowed to be.

Well, no more time to worry about that!!!

We pulled up to the house, and all the kids were quickly heading our way. I saw our other bonus son walking our way, and he was going straight to my husband to give him a big tight hug, a hug in which I knew exactly what was being said.

The fun starts and chaos breaks out. Where's T? You guys see her? I can't find that girl anywhere.

My husband comes around the corner laughing and says, *Come here quick and look at your kids.*

I looked around the corner, and there on the ground is both my full-grown bonus son and my adult daughter rolling around on the floor tickling each other like five year old kids. Then, they jumped up and started chasing each other through the house, laughing and giggling the whole time.

I glanced toward my husband, who wasn't even watching them, he was watching me watching them, and when he looked at me, for the first time I knew.

God had officially given me my promise!

The promise He made to me in that tree so very long ago. I was now living it, and all I could say was, *Thank you God, for loving me so very much*!

I looked at my husband with all the love I can hold in both my hearts, and said, *God is Good*.

My husband grabbed my hand and said, *All the Time*!

The rest of the trip was terrific, and the three of us became closer than ever, it was perfect all the way around!

Oh and YES! Uganda did hold the last pieces my girl needed to fully know, and understand the really cool Father I had been telling her all about!

The Christmas party in Uganda was the best ever, with over 1,200 kids being fed a hot meal and more than 500 adults also receiving meals.

There was music and entertainment the whole day. A bouncing house with kids crawling all over it, laughing and having fun just as children should. It was a beautiful and amazing trip, all the way around.

Time went way too fast and before we knew it, it was already time to go back home. We headed back with heavy hearts, as none of us were wanting to leave, but life keeps going, so home we went.

TIME JUMP TO CURRENT PRESENT:

Well, we're almost to the end, and you've caught up to me in the current time.

Before I go, do you remember my house guest? The one that made the house sphere go funky? Well, they are back, and since their return, it's been nothing short of an emotional roller coaster.

Let me explain that a little for you. You see, my friend is someone I told you I looked up to. And maybe that was the whole reason this all is happening. I'm not sure yet, cuz I'm still smack in the middle of it all. I have actually rewritten this part almost five times now.

Anyway, they had recently gone through a tragedy and wanted a place to go away to and heal. Of all the places they could have gone in the world, they wanted to come here, stating that they felt so much love here in my home.

I'm beaming and so thankful they feel that way. I started to get everything arranged, wanting them to feel at home, and looking forward to talking with each other.

My friend is not only my friend, but also a colleague to both my husband and me, so I had also planned to talk about some business during the visit as well.

The day after their arrival we had a lovely day talking and catching up. That evening while I was in the garage, my husband and my friend came out to have coffee with me.

Oh nice, is all my friend said, before sitting down slowly, oddly slow.

After a moment of light chatting, my husband excused himself so we could talk. It started off nice, we are friends, and it's good to be together again.

Something straight away was said that made me think, *Awesome Lord, talk about a healing trip.*

We started talking about it further, but when it should have gone deep, it didn't. Instead, it went into a light, as a matter of fact thing, and suddenly it was no big deal at all.

I sat there looking at them, now with my head tilted, and not in a good way. I shot up my prayer, slash question, *Ok Lord, something doesn't make sense, I thought I knew this person.*

I went on listening to them now doing something I dislike. Telling their story, but not for the sake of healing, no this was the famous, my past was worse than yours story. I quietly listened for a bit longer, then said it was late, and we should go back inside the house.

The next morning, my friend woke up and started towards the shower room. Stopping, they turned around, walked to me and sat down next to me on the couch.

My friend started crying and said, *It's strange in your house, I can hear God so loud here.* Then they explained that God had kept them up all night tossing and turning.

I'm smiling inside thinking, *God You Rock*! They're about to get on the pruning wagon, next stop healingville!

I replied casually, *Do you have any idea what God is trying to talk to you about?* They said no and asked how to find out.

I stopped, and then smiled saying, *I might know why you heard Him so loudly in your room. You are in our daughter's old room and my old painting room, so ya, I can understand why you heard Him so loudly in there. Maybe you go back to your room, pray to God and ask what's going on.*

They agreed, and now smiling, they went for a shower then upstairs to spend some time with God.

Waiting and waiting but then nothing is said about the situation. Not one word, they went about their day as if it had never happened.

And then, BAM!!! It suddenly went funky sphere in my house.

I prayed again and said, *I love you God, let whatever be whatever, it's your rodeo dude.*

And with that, I walked away and went back to writing. Well, trying to write. After this happened, it all got heavy in the house.

Later that day when my husband came home, he soon after said, *It's weird in the house, what's wrong with the sphere.*

Dude, I thanked God that I was no longer alone in my weird little world.

Then our daughter came home, and sure enough, soon after she came in, she says, *It's not right in the house, what's the deal?*

I'm happy inside and again thanking God that I was finally walking in life now with two more warriors who also felt the sphere immediately, *This is nice Lord, really nice.*

Well, not nice but you know what I mean.

I told my husband and daughter what happened earlier that morning and my daughter laughed out loud when I said the part about: *It's strange in your house, I can hear God so loud here.*

She laughed and said, *Oh ya, I get that.*

I laughed back and went on to say that our friend never did anything with the feeling, explaining that they shoved it aside and chose to ignore it.

I asked God, *Why don't they want to have an in-depth conversation with any of us?*

He gently replied later that evening when I was in bed, *No matter how little or how much you think someone has, never underestimate the power of...Pride*

Bummer! My friend missed a Big Moment Choice in time.

Again, I can't force them or anyone else to listen and hear God, only they can make that decision.

God did Show Up only He wasn't allowed to Show Off.

As for me, I am learning a very valuable lesson. I looked up to someone way more highly than I should have. I so badly wanted to believe what I was being told by this person.

Honestly though, I had never stopped long enough to really look at the situation in a whole.

Once I stepped back and tilted my head a little, it all looked very different.

The End

Wait! What happened with the house guest?

Sorry dude, you're now sitting next to me on my couch.
I don't know what happens next, that's the whole point.
Welcome to my rodeo!

Now that you've read it all. I would like to ask you that question from the start of the book.

Do you think choosing LOVE was worth it?

A SHOUT OUT OF THANKS

Ok, so lying in bed last night after I wrote the Horse Head Story (it's below this area) I got to thinking. What if this is the only thing I ever get to write? I mean seriously, I don't know what's coming next. This story you just read started out to be a simple three maybe a four page website and look at what happened.

I don't write, did I ever mention that? I've always wanted to, just didn't have the skills to do it, or maybe what I wanted to say wasn't that important. So ya, I have no clue what's next with this. But if this is the only chance I get, then I want to make sure and thank three key people, that have helped me become the Christian I am today and the Christian I strive to be every day forward.

With all my heart, Thank You To:
My mom Katz ~ Joyce Meyer ~ Craig Groeschel
Here let me explain that a little...

AGE 5: My Mom Katz
The first and foremost is my mom Katz. She got the most important years, the early years of my life! I told you that God came into my life at age five years old.

Well, there was a reason God did it that way, and I can never ever thank Him enough for loving me so much. Not the place here to tell it, maybe at another time.

Anyway, one awesome thing that my mom did was that she never tried to say, oh the bible means this or the bible means that. No, my mom let God raise me. See, my mom and I became Christians at about the same time. She went all in on learning, and when I had certain questions, not all but most she would simply say, *Go ask God then come back and tell me what He told you.*

I would, and He did, and I would come back and tell my mom what God told me, she would smile and say, *Well looks like you got your answer,* smiling I would reply, *Ok* and go on about my business.

Mom, thank you for understanding that it's not Nature vs. Nurture, but that it is how you Nurture the Nature that works.

My mom let me have my own very weird world with God, she didn't try to control it, she simply accepted my weirdness and let me be me.

God also gave my mom ten years to place (or rather cram) as much God in me as she could, and she did!! Oh ya, I had *that* mom! The one that was at church 24/7 if you'd let her.

Monday then again on Wednesday evening, than always something going on Saturday, then of course, Sunday morning then back again Sunday night and repeat for ten years, you get the idea.

Back then I thought it was horrible, but now I can't thank my mom enough for doing what God told her to do way back then.

Oh Man!! If I ever do get to write something again, please remind me to tell you the story: Pots, Pans & Muffin Tin.

AGE 15-23: All Me

Hot chicky day dude, did I ever mess stuff up!

At the young age of fifteen, I lost my way and started down a very dark path in life. I turned away from God, He never turned from me.

Even though I had all that God in me, I still grew up and got angry, my childhood was hard, very hard. I was used and abused from every direction, whether emotionally, physically or mentally, it was a never-ending circle for me.

Please understand, God didn't come into my life to wave a magic wand and make it all better. No, He knew what I would have to face soon, and He also knew that if I didn't hear HIS voice first, right now!

I would have had a tough time finding His soft voice later through all the screaming that was coming my way.

He did go through it all with me! Never leaving me alone, even when I told Him I never wanted to talk to Him again.

He simply sat quietly beside me and loved me normal, until I could let Him in to love me whole! I moved out of my home at the very young age of fifteen. By age twenty-three, I ended up on my bathroom floor broken inside and totally done with this world!

This was suicide request number two, I cried out to God, and He RAN to me. The next couple of years I was dazed and confused, spinning circles trying to figure out how to fix the mess I had made of my life.

AGE 25: Joyce Meyer

God put Joyce Meyer in my Face right around age twenty-five. Yes, I wrote that right, in my FACE.

I love that lady with all my heart, she's sincere and helped me unclutter my mind! She is direct and will get in your face to help you. Over the years, she shared her story, and I felt my heart drop, you mean I wasn't alone? Someone else out there had been hurt like me?

But look at her, she's got it all together. She's a preacher on TV, her life must be ok now, but how did she do that?

I really wanted to know! How did she fix her life?

I got Joyce back in the 90's when she was just starting out on TV. I was very drawn to her direct way, as it was a lot like...hhhmmm me.

All joking aside, I got addicted to her direct challenges, I'm stubborn and bull headed so she was exactly what I needed!

Please, get this! I did NOT just listen to Joyce in the morning then skip through my day. UUuuhhh no dear, I did what she told me to do! She said that even if you don't feel like it, keep doing it and doing it and doing it until you become that person.

Well, ok...so I started...

I listened to her all day / every day...all day / every day.... over and over and over and over. I played her in the house, the car, the gym, the grocery store...EVERY DAY ALL DAY!!

I need you to get this!

For a month? No.
For a year? No.
For Five years? Uuuuhhh no.
It took me more than EIGHT YEARS of over and over and over EVERY DAY ALL DAY, to tear down the walls and let God in to help make me a better person inside!!!
I'm a little hard headed, maybe a touch of stubborn ...or a lot... depending on who you ask.
The point is, I did it, and I kept doing it, it took YEARS, but I did it!
I still watch Joyce almost every day, and I read my 365-day book from her every morning, I love being raised by her! She is an amazing Bonus Mom, and I could never thank her enough for all the hard work she and her husband do!!!

Ok, now we go to the next mentor which actually overlapped with Joyce by about three maybe four years. When God brought this next mentor into my life. Dude, I kicked and screamed on this one!

AGE 26: Craig Groeschel

Oh gosh dude, this wasn't funny at all, at the time! It was about 1996ish. I'm driving outside town when I pulled up to a stop light, and there cady corner to the light was a little white building with a banner outside, not sure anymore what it said, probably something along the lines of: new church meeting here - bring your own chair....
Whatever the sign, God said, *Go there.*
I huffed and puffed and didn't care to go there, and when I walked in and saw a 'male' preacher. I tried to turn around on my heel, and walk right out!
Why? I had NO use for a MAN telling me anything to do with my life!

I hated men, I mean I hated ALL of them. I was abused for so many years, and now that deep hate wanted nothing to do with this nerdy V-neck sweater wearing, preppy dude!

Kick and yell in my head I did, but I stayed, and I watched (leered really) and did listen (a little) as this preppy guy stood up there and talked about God.

Towards the end I was starting to feel weird, I blew it off thinking, *Oh ya he's just a crackpot, and I need to get out of here. I mean all men are stupid anyway.*

The coming week and God would NOT let me stop thinking about this preppy preacher that seemed, what was that word?

Oh ya, *Sincere.*

Wait, a sincere man?

Well, that's just absolute nonsense!

Next Sunday morning in my apartment and I told God how I felt, *I will NOT listen to that man!*

Stomping around getting dressed to go back to that little white building church. I kept on going with my rant, *ALL men lie, they cheat, steal and use people, what could he possibly tell me of any value.*

Well, I went to little white building church, and I kept going, again and again, then snap, next thing you know. I'm now preacher stalking this dude.

I was now on a mission to find out this nerdy guys angle. I told myself I would prove he was like all the others, and quite frankly, God gladly accepted my mission goal. Whatever He could do to get me to just SHUT-UP already and go to church.

Well, that was 1996ish and I stayed in Life Church. I'm actually still part of Life Church this very day. I was there for the first new building. I was at a movie theater services at the mall. I was there when life groups were started, I was in one of the very first life groups that were started. I was there when the first new sister church joined from the other side of town by a big cross on a hill that I loved so much to drive by.

As I write this, it is now 2019 over twenty years later and what I am about to say next is not an exaggeration! It is true!!!

The only man to never break a promise to me is:
Craig Groeschel

It's true, from the first early days of his church in that little white building that saved my life, he's never lied to me, he's never broke a promise to me.

He has held true to who he is and has been the: faithful, loyal, trustworthy, honest and open Husband, Father and Pastor I *desperately* needed to be able to trust and depend on.

And now? Oh Ya Buddy! My husband of almost fifteen years is now not only, a real live Weird Christian, he's also currently being raised up to be the man he should be for God 1st and me 2nd.

Can you guess by who?

Yes, you guessed it: Craig Groeschel!!!

Could I ask for more? Uh NOPE! Because this has been my heart desire prayer for the last fourteen years! Never ever give up on a miracle!

I married my husband in 2004
He married me back in 2017

God is Good...All The Time
...AND...
All The Time...God Is Good!!!

If you ever happen to read this Pastor Craig, Thank you! For leading by example in how to truly be:
A Fully Devoted Follower Of Christ!

Ok Sandra, this is for you girl!

Uh Nope, the following story doesn't fit in anywhere, but you know what? A promise is a promise, and my girlfriend Sandra has always loved me special.

Let me explain. She has never understood my weird relationship with God, but you know the one thing she has never done? She has never doubted it! Quite frankly, I rather have that direct and honest relationship than the ones where people try to fake it.

Sandra is a special person to me, and she is also the friend that has said to me many times over the years, *Girl you should write a book*, I laughed it off. Another time, *I'm serious, you should write a book, but if you ever do, you must promise to tell the horse head story.*

I laughed and quickly agreed, of course thinking I would never be doing any of this.

Well, Snap! Now here I am at the end and never found a way to slide the story in for her.

I had to make a choice. I could just forget it and laugh it off the next time I see her, or I could do what I promised.

And since I have no idea if this goes anywhere or if I ever get to write again...

Love ya Sandra! Here's your story, as promised.

HORSE HEAD STORY

Ok, so I was raised in the country, way out in the country, I loved animals, and I had many animals, as well as many varieties of animals. I had a ridiculously high number of cats running around, a longhorn bull named *Bull*, and that bull loved to play tug and throw with my dad. A big black and white cow named *Pet*, she thought she was a dog and would come running when I called the dogs to dinner each night. I always laughed watching her run, because she would run her big cow body across the field like she was not a cow.

Made me laugh typing that, had a memory flash of her running towards me...hahaha

I had my faithful German Shepard (first pet I ever had, she was older by this time but still right by my side) a few other dogs that I loved just as much. A rabbit named *Stop*, because she would not jump anywhere. A three-legged turtle called *Go*, because he would never stop walking. A goat that we saved from off the side of the cliff. And that goat named *Clementine* danced every morning at 6am on the air conditioner. And then we had my welch pony named *Bonfire*. She was my best friend in the whole wide world!

I would hurry home after school so that Bonfire and I could ride the rest of the afternoon, usually not coming back until dark. We had a special place we went to. A place I wasn't supposed to ride to alone, because you had to cross a very steep valley to get there, and I was only about nine years old at the time.

If you know anything about riding horses, then you will understand this. When we went down the first part, I would have to put all my trust in her. My horse would adjust herself, look it over and then let out her huff that let me know, *Ok lay back and be very still.*

Then up the other side was just as tricky, but by now, after so many times of doing this, it was a natural movement between us.

On the other side was a beautiful open field that I loved so very much. We would play tag and run around together, yes me and my horse would play tag. I would let her run, kick and enjoy, while I would go climb trees and talk to God. Spending the afternoon finding rocks and things I thought were possible treasures.

We had to be back to the valley crossing before dark, and often it was Bonfire that let out the sound, stating that it was time to go, if it got to dark, we couldn't cross back over and would be stuck there all night.

Ya, ask me sometime, how I know that one..lol

Sometimes of course, I didn't go riding with Bonfire, either the weather was bad, or more than likely, I was in trouble and grounded from riding. Whatever the reason was this day, I'm inside and I hear Bonfire in the back whinnying out to me. I looked and nothing was wrong, so I went back to watching TV. She whinnied again, and then I got worried that she was hurt, so I went outside.

When I got to her, she nudged me and started walking me towards the house. If I stopped, she would stop, then she would look at me whinny again and walk again towards the house. I followed her and she went to the back door of the house, stopped and looked at me.

OOOohhh I get it! You want to be inside with me.

She missed me and knew I was right there in the house, and didn't understand why she couldn't come in the house with me.

Well, trust me I would have gladly let her come in the house, but seeing how just a few short weeks before I had kind of already brought a baby calf in the house and when my mom came home, I found out very fast that that was BAD.

Still rubbing my butt a little from the recent yardstick memory, I quickly recalled my mom's last words, *No more animals IN the house!* (Keyword of her sentence - IN)

So here I am, looking at my best friend who's wanting to come and watch TV with me. Yes, I know right, but it's true, my horse has watched TV with me many times before, only it was from the large front yard window. The only problem was that my dad had moved the TV, and had also made it VERY clear that I was not to move the TV, ever again.

Now what? You'd think I'd be stumped right? Haha ya right, you have no idea the little bugger I was when I was younger. Oh, the stories I could tell, as I shake my head right now. I would tell my mom sorry for it all, but she knows I'm not. We had lots of fun, right mom?!?!?

Ok, so no horse allowed in the house. Not allowed to move the TV. I'm looking around, and then it hit me. The perfect plan!

All I have to do is figure out how to get my welch pony about three or four feet off the ground by the backyard kitchen window....
Ya, you can already see where this is going? What could possibly go wrong, right?

So outside I go walking around looking for something my horse could stand on, I came around the side of the barn and bingo, there are some old square barrel thingies, if I set these side by side, lay that deal on top. *HHmm is this going to be strong enough?* I said as I started jumping up and down on my creation, *Oh ya that will be perfect*!

Ok, all lined up against the house, I stand up and, oh dangit there's a screen on the window.
Hhmmm think mom would mind if I pop this out? Ooohh surely not.
I go back inside to the kitchen planning to gently pop out the screen.

Now, I don't know if you have ever lived in or understand an old country house like mine, but ours sometimes would shock the bejeebers outta ya if you touched the metal stove stripe and the metal rim around the kitchen sink at the same time.
No? just me? Ok well, it hurts!

So, I'm trying to hurry, and in my hast, I put my hands up on each corner to jump up on the counter and ZAP!

Off I fall, rolling around on the floor knowing for sure this would be the one to kill me, and my horse is now outside the window whinnying because she has gotten tired of waiting, and is now standing on her rigged creation looking into the window wanting to know where I was.

Ok shake that off, run back outside and get her off the box, run again inside, watch the stove!

And LIGHTLY pop out the window screen, hands on both sides of the sink, feet up above me on each side of the window screen. *Ok, balance girl....and just lightly pop it out.*

Uuuhh ooopps, apparently I popped a little too hard.

I've now knocked the whole window out, glass window, metal frame and all.

My horse got startled and jumped back a little. Only now, she wants to get back on the box, and I'm flippen out afraid she's going to shatter the window glass that miraculously hadn't broken into a million pieces.

Now seeing the literal end of my life in sudden flashes I run outside. Sliding around the house corner yelling to my horse, but trying not to yell too loudly and startle her, *Easy girl... plez don't get me killed, oh man this is bad, please walk towards me girl.*

So now, my horse and I are looking at the full window that lay on the ground, and I thought fast and hard, *Now what?!?!.* Spinning for a new plan, I think and think.

And of course, another great idea pops into my head.

I decide that I'm going to just put the window back in before mom comes home. I'll just use a couple little wood slivers to slide in between the window pane creases, and hopefully the whole thing won't fall out before mom opens the window in the next days, and I can blame her.

Ok, sounds like a solid plan, I should get outta this easy enough. You have to understand, I'm the ONLY child, alone in the country!

If something goes wrong around my house, you know right away exactly who did it.

So new plan set and mom's not home for a couple more hours, I got the horse onto the rigged stand and her head now sticking all the way in the window. I'm next to her on the counter, lying against her watching TV and enjoying life, as much as possible before my mom comes home.

Uuuuhhh Hot chicky day dude! That is not a good sound my friend!!!
I heard the car door shut. NO!! Moms home!
I totally forgot the time, and my horses head is still in the window, now my best friend is refusing to leave me.
Then there's me, trying to get off the counter as fast as possible! Hands down and ZAP! I shock the bejeebers outta myself again, now rolling on the floor when the door opens...

The yelling started almost immediately, and my horse bolted fast wanting to get back to the field, smart horse.
And me? Oh dude, I was like a scared cat trying to run on a slick floor, I desperately tried to grab traction before she got to me.
I finally jumped up... just before my mom grabbed the end of my shirt and dude, I ran for my ever lovin life!!!

Running like a jackrabbit across our backyard, I looked back at my mom, now trying not to start laughing as I see her closing in on me, swinging that a yardstick that I knew all too well...

YOU PUBLISHED WITH ERRORS

Yes, I know! I'm totally twitching right now!!!
Remember this: Be very careful the agreements you make with God!
It all came down to taking a date back for me, and I didn't even catch it.
Yepper, I had a brain freeze, a full-on dduuuuur moment, if you will.
Let me explain how I got myself into this pickle mess.

If you look at the paperback version online, you will find that the
publish date is: May 7th, 2019. Well, that's a very important date for me.

You see, May 7th, 2017 was the exact date, two years before when this
whole thing started on my story that you just read.
Yep, May 7th, 2017 was when my worst nightmare started. So, now two
years later on this May 7th, 2019, I was having a bad day... I hate May 7th.

I was also up to my eyeballs in the edits for my book, listening to the
voices in my head telling me again how stupid I was even to consider doing
this publicly, knowing it's only going to take a hot second to figure out who
wrote it, and then let the judgments begin.

But whatever, right now I'm too busy fighting stupid memory flashes
from two years back. It gets easier each year, but I just really wanted
something to shove in the devil's face! You know what I mean?

Gggrrrrr did I mention that I hate May 7th?
That was all I had running through my head, and the devil knows I'm
already a little twisted up inside, and he took full advantage of the situation
and timing.

Nailed it too! Jerk had me in full emotions and not wanting to do the
book, yet again.

My eyes were hurting from all the edits I'd already done that week, and the words had all started running together. My plan was to publish that coming weekend, hence the stress I was putting on myself to get done, or so I thought anyway.

I turned off the computer and simply had a full-blown pity party moment over the actual day. I had gotten myself all upset because nothing was happening that day. I wasn't planning to leave the house and didn't see any really great possibilities for a *fancy dawning* or *amazing moment* to happen. Now convinced that it was going to be, yet another year before I could have something happen to take this day back from the devil. It just made me so stinking mad, I just wanted my stuff back and wasn't happy to wait another year.

You have got to understand that the devil took a lot from me in 2017. Not just the big and obvious things, he made sure to take away all the little things too, and to me, those LITTLE things meant, well, everything to me!

And that stupid devil had taken them from me, right down to my favorite flower! That jerk not only took my favorite flower, but he also took my favorite restaurant, my favorite vacation place, my place in the garden, my seat in the car, even my flippen place on the couch! Trust me it's way too much to explain here, but let's just say, I have been very busy taking my stuff back over the last two years, and I was almost done too!

Remember in the book, I told you that I wanted to 'take all my stuff back'? Well, I meant it!
So, on May 7th, 2019, I was flippen my lid and went off on my request, *God, how am I going to claim this day back? I really don't want to wait another year to take it back, but I don't see anything happening today.*

Not wanting to sit still, I went back to my edits hoping to be done in a few days when it hit my heart, *You have to make a choice. Do you want perfection or do you want the date?*

I popped off, *Well, I've never been perfect or cared about being perfect, so taking the date is what I want, why?*

Then the distance I had left on the book edits caught my eye. It was only 2pm in the afternoon, and it showed I was already at 85%. I could push through and just do it.

But why would I do that? It's not accurate or ready yet, I could never do that, I pushed that feeling aside thinking it was the devil messing with me, maybe, was it, was it not?

Then the date hit me!!!!

Ya duuur, I hadn't even put the two together, and honestly, it had never hit me since I had been writing for almost a month by this point.

Then again on my heart, *It's your choice, push through on the last 15% and take the date back, or get the edits perfect and wait until next year.*

I didn't like those choices at all.

See, I really am perfectionist, and I had already spent a lot of money for someone to edit my book, but they didn't understand my Mid-West Okie Slang and when I got it back.

Dude! It was a mess, they had tried to change everything that was me, and then I got utterly confused when I tried to go through their edits, to put it into my edits, and well, it all got messed up.

I had spent the last days trying to fix it. I know my grammar is off, and I also know that I talk hick and that I write like I talk, it is what it is.

Long story short, I had to make a choice between the perfection of the book, which meant wait another year to take my date back, or push through and take my date back now.

I got really scared when I was about to hit the *send* button at almost 11pm on the night of May 7th. I was twitching and wiggling around not wanting to, knowing I'll soon be judged for the errors.

I then quickly tried, one last time, to get out of it by saying, *Maybe I should hold off. I mean what if they can't even read it?*

God made me laugh so hard with his reply, *Have you read the texts from your kids lately?*

Well, with that... I laughed out loud, hit the button and took my date back!

My Father asked me to do this, and I did it.
I can't live for any other approval than His.

He's happy with my heart, so I'm satisfied with this book, as is.

www.ingramcontent.com/pod-product-compliance
Lightning Source LLC
Chambersburg PA
CBHW021130020426
42331CB00005B/699